LIGUORI CHRISTIAN INITIATION PR

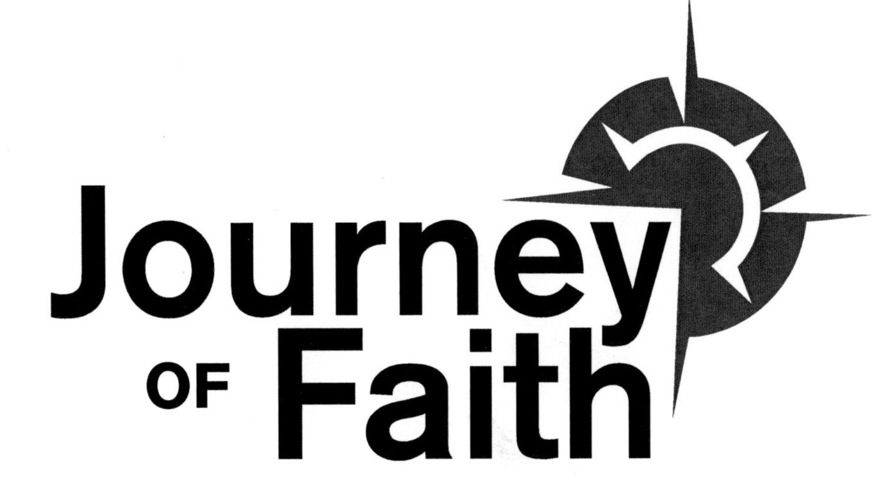

INQUIRY LEADER GUIDE

Journey of Faith for Teens, Inquiry Leader Guide (826306)

Imprimi Potest: Stephen T. Rehrauer, CSsR, Provincial, Denver Province, the Redemptorists

Imprimatur: "In accordance with CIC 827, permission to publish has been granted on May 25, 2016, by the Most Reverend Edward M. Rice, Auxiliary Bishop, Archdiocese of St. Louis. Permission to publish is an indication that nothing contrary to Church teaching is contained in this work. It does not imply any endorsement of the opinions expressed in the publication; nor is any liability assumed by this permission."

Journey of Faith © 1993, 2005, 2016 Liguori Publications, Liguori, MO 63057.
To order, visit Liguori.org or call 800-325-9521.

Liguori Publications, a nonprofit corporation, is an apostolate of the Redemptorists. To learn more about the Redemptorists, visit Redemptorists.com. All rights reserved. No part of this publication may be reproduced, distributed, stored, transmitted, or posted in any form by any means without prior written permission.

Text: Adapted from *Journey of Faith for Adults* © 2000 Liguori Publications.
Editor of 2016 edition: Theresa Nienaber. Design: Lorena Mitre Jimenez. Images: Shutterstock.

Unless noted, Scripture texts in this work are taken from the *New American Bible*, revised edition © 2010, 1991, 1986, 1970 Confraternity of Christian Doctrine, Washington, DC, and are used by permission of the copyright owner. All Rights Reserved. No part of the *New American Bible* may be reproduced in any form without permission in writing from the copyright owner. Excerpts from English translation of the *Catechism of the Catholic Church* for the United States of America © 1994 United States Catholic Conference, Inc.—*Libreria Editrice Vaticana*; English translation of the *Catechism of the Catholic Church: Modifications from the Editio Typica* © 1997 United States Catholic Conference, Inc.—*Libreria Editrice Vaticana*. Excerpts from *The Rites of the Catholic Church, Volume One* [abbreviated *RCIA* herein] © 1990 Liturgical Press.

Compliant with *The Roman Missal, Third Edition.*

Printed in the United States of America
27 26 25 24 23 / 7 6 5 4 3
Third Edition

The process by which adults are initiated into the Catholic faith throughout the United States is now called the OCIA—the Order of Christian Initiation of Adults. "Order" is a clearer translation of the Latin term for the process formerly known as the RCIA—the Rite of Christian Initiation of Adults. People preparing for baptism and reception into the Church celebrate several rites as part of the order to which those rites belong—an order whose mission is to journey in the faith. The US Conference of Catholic Bishops adopted the name change in 2021, with American dioceses introducing the name thereafter. For more information, please contact your local diocese.

Contents

Welcome to *Journey of Faith*!

Liguori Publications is dedicated to providing parishes with quality resources like *Journey of Faith*. Since 1993, *Journey of Faith* has established itself as a trusted and beloved program for catechists to guide participants through the OCIA process. As the Catholic Church takes on the challenges and graces of each generation, *Journey of Faith* has been carefully developed to help you meet the changing needs of adults, teens, and children who are inquiring about and seeking initiation into the Catholic Church—ever ancient, ever new.

One new aspect of the journey is the name of the OCIA process. It is now called the Order of Christian Initiation of Adults (OCIA). "Order" reflects a new translation of the Latin term for the process formerly known as the Rite of Christian Initiation of Adults. People preparing for baptism and reception into the Church celebrate several rites as part of the order to which those rites belong—an order whose mission is to journey in the faith. The US Conference of Catholic Bishops adopted the change in November 2021. Your local diocese has more information.

The *Journey of Faith* program is cohesive, comprehensive, and flexible. The Word Into Life provides you with the *Lectionary* texts from Sunday Mass, and the forty-eight catechetical lessons and corresponding *Leader Guides* create a practical and attractive formation process for today's team leaders, catechists, and participants. All the materials are referenced to the *Catechism of the Catholic Church* and have been granted an *imprimatur* from the Archdiocese of St. Louis.

Unbaptized children over the age of seven are to be considered catechumens. Liguori offers any child or teen needing formation or sacraments *Journey of Faith for Children* and *Journey of Faith for Teens*. With the exception of the *Word Into Life* volumes, all *Journey of Faith* products are available in Spanish under the title *Jornada de fe*.

We hope you enjoy using *Journey of Faith* and find it enlightening and engaging for all. To see our entire collection of sacramental preparation titles, parish subscriptions, formation and spirituality books, and more, please visit Liguori.org to contact us for a copy of the latest catalog.

—The editors

An Overview of the OCIA

The Historical Development

The decision to become a member of the early Christian community bore serious ramifications. Becoming Christian meant a break with one's background and often required fracturing relationships with the non-Christian members of one's family. In many cases, this decision meant a willingness to suffer persecution or even death, as seen in the example of the martyrs Perpetua and Felicity. Perpetua, a noblewoman of Carthage and mother of an infant son, and Felicity, a pregnant slave woman, both refused to denounce Christianity and were subsequently martyred during the public games in the amphitheater around AD 200.

Just as the decision to become a Christian was not made lightly, the formation process wasn't quick or easy. Catechumens—those in the process of preparing for baptism—were invited into a step-by-step journey of three or more years with the community before achieving full membership. During this process, they were expected not only to begin to accept Christian beliefs but also to begin to live the Christian life. The community shared their faith with the catechumens and celebrated each step along with them.

One period of this preparation has remained throughout the centuries: Lent. Originally this time was one of immediate preparation for baptism, which was celebrated at the Easter Vigil. During Lent, the entire Christian community, especially the catechumens, devoted themselves to prayer, fasting, and self-scrutiny. For those already baptized, it was a time to remember and renew their original commitment.

During the solemn Easter Vigil, the catechumens—now called the elect—received the sacraments of initiation (baptism, confirmation, and Eucharist) and were welcomed into the community. As a rule, this initiation was celebrated at the Easter Vigil only. Formation of the newly baptized did not end with the rites of Holy Saturday night, however, but continued with further instruction and daily living out of Christian values.

This process began to change in the fourth century, when periodic persecution of Christians was replaced by tolerance. Because of the favor many emperors showed toward it, Christianity became fashionable, and many people began entering the catechumenate for social and political reasons. As a result, the pattern and standards for formation gradually transitioned to the point where, by the fifth century, the rites of initiation were separated into the three sacraments we know and celebrate today. Infant baptism became the norm, and the catechumenate vanished.

The Church published the first *Roman Catechism* in 1566, following the Council of Trent. This book of teachings was presented in question-and-answer form and was used for instruction of the faithful. Such catechisms later became the foundation for what came to be called "convert classes." Using a teacher-student model, the priest would meet with interested parties and assist them in memorizing certain prayers and learning the material in the catechism. The duration of the process, the material to be covered, and the format were left to the priest or parish custom, with few outside directives given.

Successful completion of these classes meant either baptism or formal reception into the Catholic Church. This event was usually celebrated in a private ceremony, with only close family in attendance. Those received into the Church would be confirmed by the bishop at the cathedral or would receive the sacrament in their local parish whenever the bishop came to confirm the schoolchildren. Follow-up for the new Catholics, if any, might consist of being sent to a formal course in liturgy, Scripture, dogma, or morality.

Following World War II, a call for a change in the formation of new Catholics came from the Church in Africa. They began to use the ancient form of the catechumenate to provide stability in formation and a period of time for faith to mature. The Second Vatican Council in the 1960s called for a thorough revision of all the rites (Constitution on the Sacred Liturgy *[Sacrosanctum Concilium]*, 4), and a committee was formed that engaged in a formal study and revision of the methods leading to baptism or reception into the Catholic Church. This study resulted in the promulgation of the *Rite of Christian Initiation of Adults* (*RCIA*) in 1972. (See page 4 to see why the name of the process changed in 2021.)

Thus the catechumenate was restored: a process of formation, sanctified by various liturgical rites that mark progress in the journey of faith and culminate in full membership in the Catholic Christian community. An integral part of the revision is that the whole process and its rites are to be celebrated with and in the context of the local parish community and diocese.

The Scholastic or Ongoing Catechumenal Model

The catechumenate is considered a *process*, rather than a *program*, because it is a spiritual journey that varies according to time, place, and individual needs. It primarily focuses on:

- *Faith development* (rather than mastery of doctrine) and maturing in one's relationship with God.
- *Building and nourishing relationships,* not only among the participants and leaders but within the parish community and the universal Church.

Most U.S. parishes follow an academic schedule that begins in September and runs through May. However, this approach can make the process feel forced, rushed, or like a course of study that focuses on the *content* of the faith rather than the participant's experience of a *deepening conversion* and growing commitment. For this and other reasons (for example, risking that the *Catechism* becomes the main "course text" rather than the *Lectionary*), many pastoral ministers prefer an ongoing model for the process. *Journey of Faith* can be applied well to a number of models and provides a built-in flexibility that supports many formats.

Flexibility is one of the greatest assets of the OCIA. Within certain parameters, the pastor is given the freedom to accommodate the rites according to his judgment in order to fit the needs of the participants and parish. You, as catechists and team leaders, are encouraged to use your judgment in developing a process suited to the needs of both catechumens and candidates.

The Periods

This section provides detailed information on the periods of the OCIA. A basic orientation to the OCIA process is included in lessons Q1, "Welcome to the OCIA," and C1, "The OCIA Process and Rites." Together these lessons build a foundation for the participants as they begin their faith formation. The corresponding lesson plans support you, the leader, and offer program-specific notes.

Evangelization and Precatechumenate (Inquiry)

The first period is called *inquiry* or the *precatechumenate*. During this period, inquirers form relationships with one another and with their catechists. The sessions are informal and often center upon the life stories that have led each member there with questions such as:

- What is faith?
- Who is God, and why does God care about me?
- How does the Church understand the Bible and the sacraments?
- What are the roles of Mary and the pope?
- Why are there statues in Catholic churches?

Each inquirer will examine the Church and the ways in which its members worship together and live the Christian faith. First impressions of the parish and of all involved are very important. The period culminates in the inquirer's decision to enter the catechumenate, the period of formal preparation for entrance into full membership in the Catholic Church.

Catechumenate

The *rite of acceptance* marks the beginning of the catechumenate, a period of study and reflection on the faith. At this point, the inquirers become catechumens. Candidates (those already baptized but preparing for full membership in the Catholic Church) formally enter the OCIA process through the *rite of welcoming*. Both publicly state their intention to continue their formation, and the community supports them in their journey. Sponsors will act as companions and models of faith and lend their personal support.

The length of this period is determined by the needs of each participant and of the community. It can last anywhere from several months to a couple of years. During this time, the catechumens and candidates:

- learn Catholic beliefs
- are exposed to various forms of prayer
- join the community in worship, social events, and charitable activities
- participate in the apostolic life of the Church.

During the catechumenate, catechesis usually takes place during the Sunday liturgy. The participants are prayerfully dismissed after the Universal Prayer (Prayers of the Faithful); the catechists, and sometimes the sponsors, join them in reflecting upon the day's readings and connecting them to their faith and the life of the Church (see section *The Word Into Life*).

> *There should be celebrations of the word of God that accord with the liturgical season and that contribute to the instruction of the catechumens and the needs of the community...Celebrations of the word may also be held in connection with catechetical or instructional meetings of the catechumens, so that these will occur in a context of prayer*
>
> *RCIA* chapter of *The Rites, Volume One (RCIA), 81, 84*

Purification and Enlightenment

When the catechumens and candidates are ready to make a formal request for the sacraments of initiation, and when the catechists and godparents are ready to recommend them to the bishop and to the parish community for full membership, the *rite of election* is celebrated. This celebration is generally held on the first Sunday of Lent. The rite of election marks the beginning of the *period of purification and enlightenment*, the time of immediate preparation for initiation or full reception at the Easter Vigil. (*Journey of Faith* refers to this period simply as enlightenment.)

The beginning of Lent signals a forty-day "retreat" in which the parish joins the elect in preparing for the mysteries celebrated at the Easter Vigil. The OCIA sessions are marked by increased emphasis on prayer and the interior life rather than on accumulation of knowledge. Many parishes allow time for a day of prayer especially designed for the elect and their supporters. On the third, fourth, and fifth Sundays of Lent, the scrutinies are celebrated during the liturgy. These rites are prayers of healing in which the elect, as well as the faithful, are reminded that everyone needs continued healing, conversion, and reconciliation.

Postbaptismal Catechesis (Mystagogy)

The Easter Vigil does not mark the end of the OCIA process but the beginning of a commitment to a lifelong discovery and living out of the Catholic Christian tradition. The fifty days from Easter to Pentecost are called the period of *mystagogy*, a Greek word meaning "entering into the mysteries." In the early Church, this time was used to explain the mysteries of the sacraments. Today this period serves as a time for today's neophytes (newly converted) to:

- continue to gather, pray, and nourish their faith
- deepen their experiential understanding of God's word and the sacraments
- center more on the apostolic or social justice aspects of Catholic Christianity
- claim a new role of service in the community. (All Catholics are invited to active participation in parish life, which includes worship, stewardship, and fellowship.)

Sponsors and Godparents in OCIA

"A person to be baptized is to be given a sponsor who assists an adult in Christian initiation...A sponsor also helps the baptized person to lead a Christian life...."

Code of Canon Law 872

Prior to the rite of acceptance, (OCIA) sponsors should be chosen for all catechumens. Sponsors represent the parish community and assist the larger Church in preparing the catechumen for baptism (here, initiation), testifying to his or her faith, and promising to assist him or her in living the Catholic faith.

Canon 874 lists the basic criteria for sponsors. These guidelines are the same for baptismal godparents and confirmation sponsors, though the roles are somewhat different:

1. The sponsor should be designated or invited by the catechumen or candidate. If he or she doesn't have someone in mind, the OCIA leader(s) or pastor will select an appropriate person from a voluntary pool of parishioners. This is similar to parents choosing godparents at the time of their child's baptism.
2. The sponsor must be at least sixteen years old—in other words, mature enough to understand and fulfill this important role.
3. The sponsor must be a confirmed Catholic "who leads a life of faith"—someone who has already committed to and experienced the Catholic faith journey.
4. No sponsor can be subject to a Church penalty such as excommunication.
5. The sponsor cannot be the participant's parent. In the case of infant baptism, the parents already have a unique and important role to play. Some adult catechumen desire to have their spouse or a close friend or relative as a sponsor. This is generally discouraged, but OCIA leaders and pastors can help the catechumen decide whether the potential sponsor is sufficiently experienced and objective to fulfill this role.

OCIA leaders should develop a list of parishioners who are willing to become sponsors and maintain those connections as new inquirers arrive each year. It is important for sponsors with no prior relationship to the catechumen to realize that they are committing to an *ongoing* spiritual relationship. While their ecclesial role technically ends at the rite of election, sponsors often serve as, or stand in for, godparents, whose support lasts a lifetime.

Godparents are chosen before the rite of election (*RCIA* 123). Like sponsors, they will encourage, inspire, and even hold the elect accountable to remain faithful to Christ. Whenever possible, encourage the catechumens to use their OCIA sponsor as a baptismal godparent. Additional guidance for godparents can be found in the *Journey of Faith for Teens, Catechumenate Leader Guide*.

The Rites

Rite of Acceptance Into the Order of Catechumens

This rite marks the first transition in one's journey—the move from being an interested inquirer to an active catechumen. (For candidates seeking full communion in the Church, the *rite of welcoming* is used. *RCIA* 507 and the following details the combined rite.) The importance of this step is rightly recognized by the Church.

1. Symbolizing movement into the community, those asking to be received, along with their sponsors, begin by standing at the doors of the church (*RCIA* 48). The celebrant introduces them to the worshiping community, and asks, "What do you ask of the Church?" They state their desire for initiation, implying their intent to live, learn, and love with the community.
2. The sign of the cross is marked on each forehead, symbolizing the love and strength of Christ that accompanies each person (*RCIA* 54–55). This sign of faith may also be marked on their:

a. ears (to hear the Lord's voice),
b. eyes (to see God's glory),
c. lips (to respond to God's word),
d. heart (that Christ may dwell there),
e. shoulders (to bear the gentle yoke of Christ),
f. hands (that their work witnesses to Christ), and
g. feet (to walk in Christ's way) (*RCIA* 56).

3. After the signing, catechumens and sponsors are formally invited to enter the church and to join in the celebration of the Liturgy of the Word (*RCIA* 60). Following the homily, the catechumens should be called forward and dismissed with a book of the Gospels or a cross (*RCIA* 64). They are specially included in the Mass' intercessory prayers before being formally dismissed from the assembly in order to pray and reflect upon the Scriptures (*RCIA* 65–67).

Other Rites in the Catechumenate

Other liturgical rites during this period, although optional, are significant to the continuing faith development of both participants and parishes:

- celebrations of the word of God (*RCIA* 81–89)
- minor exorcisms (*RCIA* 90–93)
- blessings (*RCIA* 95–96)
- anointing (*RCIA* 98–101)
- sending (*RCIA* 106–17)

Rite of Election

The importance of this rite is accented by the fact that it is often celebrated by the bishop (or bishop's representative) at the diocesan cathedral. The transition is marked further by a change of title and in the selection of the godparent(s) beforehand.

After the catechumens have been presented to the bishop and approved by the assembly (*RCIA* 130–31), their names are inscribed in the *Book of the Elect* (*RCIA* 132). Intercessory prayers and a special blessing for the elect follow this sacred moment.

The Scrutinies

1. The first scrutiny takes place on the third Sunday of Lent. Its focus is the story of the Samaritan woman at the well (John 4:5–42). After special intercessory prayers, the celebrant prays that the elect may be exorcised from the powers of sin (*RCIA* 150–156). During the week that follows, the presentation of the Creed should be formally made, preferably after a homily within Mass (*RCIA* 157–163).

2. The second scrutiny takes place on the fourth Sunday of Lent. It focuses on the story of the man born blind (John 9:1–41). Again, after the intercessions, the celebrant prays that the elect may be exorcised from the powers of sin (*RCIA* 164–170).

3. The fifth Sunday of Lent brings the Third Scrutiny. This Sunday focuses on the raising of Lazarus (John 11:1–45). Intercessory prayers from the worshiping community and prayers of exorcism from the celebrant again follow (*RCIA* 171–177). During the following week, the Presentation of the Lord's Prayer should be made, preferably after the reading of the Lord's Prayer from Matthew's Gospel. Following the homily, the celebrant calls on the community to pray silently for the elect. Before their dismissal, the celebrant bestows a special blessing upon the elect (*RCIA* 178–184).

Rites of Preparation

When it's possible to bring the elect together on Holy Saturday for reflection and prayer, these rites may be used in immediate preparation for the reception of the sacraments (*RCIA* 185 and following). If the *presentation of the Creed* or the *presentation of the Lord's Prayer* has not been celebrated already, they could be celebrated now. An *ephphetha rite* (a rite of opening the ears and mouth, symbolizing the hearing and proclaiming of the word) is a fitting preparation rite, as is the rite of *choosing a baptismal name*. Any or all of these rites serve to set the stage for the highlight of the OCIA experience: the sacraments of initiation.

Sacraments of Initiation

After months or years of sharing the faith, the OCIA journey culminates in this very special parish celebration. Holy Saturday is the night to celebrate, and the Church celebrates in style. In the early Church the Easter Vigil lasted until dawn; today's vigil lasts only a few hours (depending on the parish, generally between two and four). It is the most glorious celebration of the entire liturgical year.

1. This night begins in total darkness. The parish community may assemble outside for the blessing of the fire. Then, as the celebrant processes into the church, proclaiming the *Light of Christ*, each person lights a taper from the new Easter candle that has been blessed and ignited with the new fire. Soon the church is aglow with flame.

2. The Liturgy of the Word begins in candlelight. There are seven readings from the Old Testament provided, but it is not necessary to proclaim all seven. Psalms are interspersed between each reading.

3. Before the New Testament epistle is read, the "*Gloria*" rings out, the altar candles and electric lights are lit, and the Church bells are joyously rung. With this, the glorious "*Alleluia*," the Gospel, and the homily, the stage is set for the sacraments of initiation.

4. The rite of baptism begins with the calling forth of those to be baptized. A litany of the saints follows, and the celebrant blesses the water by plunging the Easter candle into the baptismal pool. Baptism follows, and the newly baptized are clothed in white garments.

5. Once the baptisms are concluded, the candidates are called forward to profess their belief in the holy Catholic Church. They join the newly baptized, and the rite of confirmation is celebrated with the laying on of hands and anointing with chrism. Then the whole assembly renews their baptismal vows and the celebrant ritually sprinkles everyone with the newly blessed waters of baptism.

6. The Mass continues with the Universal Prayer and Liturgy of the Eucharist. When it's time to receive Communion, the new Catholics—along with their godparents, sponsors, catechists, and family members—lead the congregation in the eucharistic feast. This is the culmination of initiation: sharing at the table and being sent forth.

Traits of an Effective OCIA Team Member or Catechist

You don't have to be a theology professor or an experienced minister to be a successful catechist. Certain traits and techniques can make the process of faith formation easier and more enjoyable.

- ***Meet regularly throughout the process.*** Several weeks before the start of a new program or upon the arrival of a new inquirer, review the materials and determine where and when to hold the sessions. Good planning ensures that the process goes smoothly.

- ***Be flexible.*** Resist the temptation to create a precise schedule. Remain open to the workings of the Spirit in those who present themselves. Each session should include an opportunity for unfinished or previous business to be addressed. Often questions come up between sessions that were not apparent during your time together.

- ***Make each team member aware of the topics discussed***, materials covered, and questions raised in each session so there will be continuity among sessions and presenters. Contact the next session's presenters and brief them on any issues that surfaced or may need to be addressed.

- ***Link your presentations and discussions to their life experience***. Catechists and team members are co-learners, catalysts, and partners—not directors. Openly sharing the stories of your own faith journey makes the participants more comfortable in accepting and sharing who and where they are.

- ***Be attentive and receptive.*** Communication, especially active listening, is one of your greatest tools in establishing trust. Look at the person and give him or her your undivided attention. Try to hear and to be open to what is said as well as any feelings underneath.

- ***Practice empathy and sensitivity.*** This requires a compassionate attitude and an awareness of your reactions and prejudices. Accept and affirm the uniqueness of each individual and genuinely desire to feel *with* him or her. The rest of the group will follow your example.

- ***Take advantage of opportunities for renewal and training.*** Faith is a relationship. While routines and habits are helpful, don't live by a script. Remain open to the opportunities and creative diversions of the Spirit. Above all, make time for your own spiritual growth. Take time daily for prayer. Practice the faith you share. Grow in Christ. Stay informed on new teachings and trends in the Church. Attend retreats and seminars and read books that develop your understanding and ministry skills. Be as present in the sacraments and active in the life of the parish as you hope your catechumens and candidates will be.

- ***Form a hospitality team.*** This team will provide snacks and beverages at each session and a well-planned and generously provided menu for the Easter Vigil retreat. This team does not need to stay for the sessions. In fact, they may wish to remain anonymous until the retreat, which becomes an opportunity for team members to reveal themselves and Christ's love in action.

- ***Establish an intercessory team.*** Have parishioners sign up to become a prayer partner, a secret intercessor who promises to pray for a particular catechumen or candidate throughout the OCIA process.

Traits of an Effective OCIA Sponsor

There is no one way to be a good sponsor, but certain qualities do increase a sponsor's potential. These qualities will help you recruit, maintain, and even *be* a better sponsor:

- ***A sponsor is willing to share the faith.*** A sponsor should talk with his or her catechumen about his or her faith, love, commitment, and relationship with Jesus Christ. This person shares simple ways to put our faith into words and actions to help the catechumen deepen his or her relationship with Jesus.

- ***A sponsor is prayerful.*** A sponsor has and knows the importance of an active prayer life and prays for his or her catechumen. This person is aware of and sensitive to the many different ways of praying. He or she may even teach the catechumen how to pray.

- ***A sponsor is welcoming and hospitable.*** A good sponsor makes his or her catechumen feel comfortable in and around the parish. Whether at an OCIA session, Mass, or another parish function, this person goes out of the way to greet the catechumen, sit and visit with him or her, and introduce him or her to others.

- ***A sponsor is a good listener.*** All catechumens are seeking God in one way or another. Some are very forthcoming with their story and questions; others are more reluctant. Sometimes what is *not* said is just as revealing. A good sponsor remains available, respects privacy, and listens as much (if not more) than he or she talks.

- ***A sponsor is understanding and supportive.*** A sponsor tries to understand the catechumen's feelings, concerns, joys, and uncertainties. This person shows empathy and compassion no matter what is going on and how the person feels. If something serious arises, he or she can refer the catechumen to the OCIA coordinator or pastor.

- ***A sponsor is informed and involved.*** Good sponsors help their catechumen by staying informed of news and events not only in the parish and the OCIA but also in the larger and universal Church. This person reads the bulletin, follows the Church in the media, and keeps track of the OCIA schedule. Better yet, he or she attends every session possible and obtains copies of the material to share in the experience and renew his or her own understanding.

- ***A sponsor is willing to challenge.*** If a catechumen shows a lack of commitment, serious hesitation, or resistance to the process, the sponsor should ask kindly about the situation. Being honest and willing to talk about potential conflicts will ensure the spiritual well-being and best interests of the catechumen and the Church. The OCIA coordinator or pastor may know the best way to address difficult situations.

Integrating the Parish Community

The OCIA process can renew the entire parish. It is a constant reminder of our roots, our heritage, and our traditions. Each beginning offers an opportunity for all to revisit their own journey of faith, to share how God is with us, and to mature in our relationships with God and each other. When expressed through the life of the parish, the OCIA can facilitate a continuous conversion process throughout the community and an ever clearer image of the reign of God.

- Provide OCIA updates for the parish bulletin, newsletter, or website, sharing ways parishioners can help the group and introducing them to the names and faces of the participants (see also hospitality and intercessory teams).
- Post the names of catechumens and candidates in the adoration chapel to remind visitors to intercede for OCIA participants.
- As you approach the rite of election, post photos of the OCIA participants in the vestibule or narthex of church to remind the parish to welcome and pray for the group.
- Invite parish groups and committees to send an encouraging letter to the group. These could include an introduction to their membership or ministry as well as a special gift:
    - A men's or women's group might provide journals or writing utensils.
    - The rosary group might send rosaries for the lesson on Catholic prayers and practices.
    - The fish friers or food-pantry volunteers might provide snacks for each session.
    - The altar guild or maintenance crew might deliver flowers for the room each month.

Discerning Individual Needs

No one can predict the makeup of an OCIA group. The variety of ages, backgrounds, and catechetical needs within any group, year, or parish can be huge.

Religious Heritage and Formation Level

Participants will come to you from a variety of faith backgrounds. Some may have had no faith formation or have little, if any, concept of Church, faith, and salvation. Others may have inherited biases against certain Church teachings. You may have someone who was baptized and active in another Christian denomination and someone who was baptized Catholic but not raised in the Church.

While catechumens and candidates can usually participate in the sessions together, the lived experiences of an active Christian and an unbaptized or uncatechized adult make for very different perspectives. In the celebration of the rites, the reality of baptism must be evidenced, so during the rites these two groups may need to be separated as a way of addressing their separate needs and backgrounds. Effective entrance questions and strong communications among the OCIA leaders, sponsors, and pastor should prevent critical surprises and lead each participant to initiation or full reception into the universal Church.

Be careful not to generate a one-size-fits-all process. As you prepare for each session, cater the discussions, questions, and activities to each group's needs. If you anticipate a strong interest in a subject or benefit to highlighting certain aspects of Catholic teaching or practice, do so with prudence, charity, and guidance from your pastor.

Personal Commitments and Situations

Many teens come to the OCIA process with a strong internal desire to learn about the Catholic faith, others may participate out of insistence from their parents or other outside sources. Some struggle to accept the process amid current lifestyle choices or objections to Christian moral teaching and social justice. Others may face obstacles to regular attendance or full participation—variable part-time work schedules, an overabundance of extracurriculars or schoolwork, limited access to transportation, or medical or physical challenges. Here your loving response is essential in guiding each participant in his or her faith journey.

Each participant has human dignity and is created in the image of God. Most of us have been affected by sin, whether our own or that of others, but all of us are called to conversion and new life. Use the OCIA process and other parish resources to provide the time, support, and environment each participant requires.

How to Use *Journey of Faith*

Journey of Faith consists of:

- *Forty-eight* catechetical lessons
- *Three Leader Guides*: Inquiry, Catechumenate, and Enlightenment and Mystagogy
- Three volumes of *The Word Into Life*: one for each of the Sunday cycles (Years A, B, and C)

Catechetical Lessons (Handouts)

Journey of Faith is presented in forty-eight personal, engaging, and manageable lessons so that uncatechized or nominally catechized teens can hear the good news. The lessons are divided according to the four periods of initiation:

- Sixteen ***Inquiry*** (Q#) lessons broadly cover basic questions in areas such as: what is faith, revelation, prayer, the Bible, and the meaning of the Mass and Catholic practices.
- Sixteen ***Catechumenate*** (C#) lessons address more catechetical aspects of our faith: the Church, the sacraments, the moral life, and so forth.
- Eight ***Enlightenment*** (E#) lessons focus on preparing the elect for the various rites, especially the sacraments of initiation, and guide them through Lenten themes and events.
- Eight ***Mystagogy*** (M#) lessons redirect the focus of new Catholics from learning to living.

In each lesson you will find:

- "In Short": a brief list of statements outlining the main ideas
- an explanation of a faith topic
- related Scripture and *Catechism* references
- quotes and reflections from Church documents, Catholic writings, and the saints
- questions for reflection and discussion
- an interactive activity and journaling prompt that applies the concepts and engages the group
- integrated images, icons, and sidebars throughout the program.

The tables of contents and following schedules provide an effective and logical order for a typical parish-based OCIA process. You can also follow the themes of the *Lectionary* readings, supporting them with these handouts as indicated in *The Word Into Life* (see below). Because the topics and themes are closely connected and recur throughout the *Journey of Faith* program and liturgical year, the handouts and *Leader Guides* can serve as ongoing tools. We understand that time is limited and that questions and issues arise. Ultimately, how you use the material depends on you, your parish, and the needs of each participant.

Distributing the handout prior to the session allows participants to reflect on the topic and respond to the questions ahead of time. Both the handouts and the *Leader Guides* are designed to walk you through the sessions and facilitate discussions, highlighting and reinforcing essential points along the way.

Leader Guides

To help you present each topic and prepare for the sessions, each *Journey of Faith Leader Guide* provides a lesson plan for each catechetical handout within its respective period and an alphabetical glossary of terms contained in those lessons. When used sequentially as a set, this creates a comprehensive OCIA program that is adaptable to any parish and group of participants. Along with the schedules and supply lists in this *Inquiry Leader Guide*, *Journey of Faith* equips OCIA leaders to engage participants and their sponsors in the process of conversion and faith formation.

Each lesson plan is designed to fill a ninety-minute session, not including any liturgical celebrations. As session times may vary, the material in each lesson plan can be adapted to your specific needs. Continuously assess your participants' understanding and tailor your presentation to what the group needs.

In addition to the complete participant lesson, leaders will find instructions, background information, notes, and more under these headings:

Catechism	sections of the *Catechism of the Catholic Church* covered by that lesson, and a key quote selected from the list.
Objectives	learning goals; what participants should know and be able to do after the session.
Leader Meditation	brief reflections, questions, and prayers on a Scripture passage related to the lesson's topic (see information at right).
Related *Catholic Updates* [see Adults Leader Guides]	suggested issues of the parish newsletter from Liguori Publications that explores Catholic teaching and tradition. Supplementing the handout with these articles, especially if shared with the parish congregation, promotes greater understanding by all the faithful.
Leader Preparation	tips and reminders to guide the presenter's preparation for the session, including a list of that lesson's vocabulary and special supplies.
Welcome	reminders and ideas for the beginning of a session, whether transitioning from a Liturgy of the Word or settling the group in.
Opening Scripture	a reading from Scripture that sets the context and supports the lesson's topic and discussion.
Discussion of Lesson Handout	points, prompts, suggested responses, and additional references for the leader, organized by section.
Journaling and/or **Activity**	instructions and reminders for the journaling prompt(s) and/or a summative activity.
Closing Prayer	prompts or texts to end the session in prayer.
Take-home or **Looking Ahead**	exercises that participants complete between sessions to deepen and apply their formation. Leaders should instruct participants prior to each departure and follow up as needed.

Preparing With Scripture

Before each session, catechists and team members should read the Scripture passage for that lesson as well as review the lesson plan and any accompanying catechetical material. As you reflect on the passage, consider these questions:

- Become part of the narrative. What stories of your own faith journey come to mind?
- What questions are raised in your mind?
- What are the sights, sounds, and feelings that emerge?
- What are the names and stories of the key individuals?
- What are the connections, if any, between the passage and the lesson's topic? Between the passage and other Bible readings, especially those for Sunday Mass?
- How does this passage apply to today's Church and Christian living?
- If you have time, read a devotion or commentary on the passage to deepen your understanding.

If needed, adjust the session's timing or focus to maximize your catechumens' and candidates' success with the material. After your lesson is set, relax and enjoy the opportunity to share your faith with those who are eager to be touched by God's Spirit.

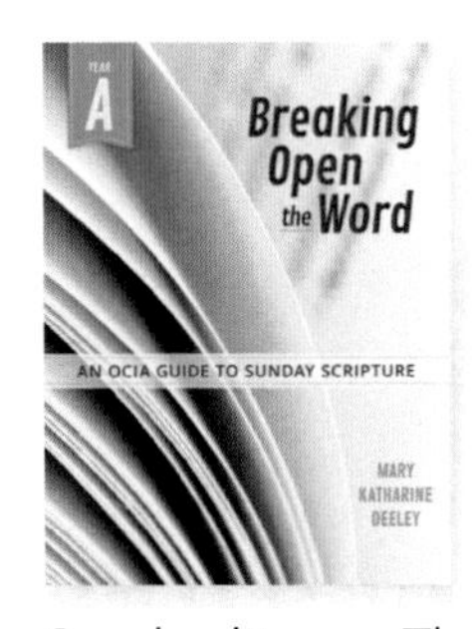

Breaking Open the Word: An OCIA Guide to Sunday Scripture

Breaking Open the Word: An OCIA Guide to Sunday Scripture assists leaders of adult and teen Christian initiation, as well as Bible study groups, to "break open" and explore the word of God proclaimed in the Sunday liturgy. The pastoral commentary and reflection questions by Biblical scholar Mary Katharine Deeley facilitate meditation and discussion, bringing Scripture alive and making it relevant to today.

Breaking Open the Word can be used on its own or in combination with Liguori Publications' *Journey of Faith* OCIA program. Each liturgy is cross-referenced to a *Journey of Faith* lesson, enabling a Lectionary-based approach to catechesis for Christian initiation.

Separate volumes of *Breaking Open the Word* are available for each liturgical cycle.
Each volume of *Breaking Open the Word* also features:

- The lectionary readings for all Sundays of the liturgical year, Advent through the Feast of Christ the King
- Readings for the third, fourth, and fifth Sundays of Lent for use when the Scrutinies are celebrated with the Elect
- The lectionary readings for the Easter Triduum
- The lectionary readings for those occasional Sunday feasts that supersede Ordinary Time celebrations
- A collection of brief gathering prayers and dismissal prayers for each phase of the initiation process

The Word Into Life: A Guide for Group Reflection on Sunday Scripture

The liturgy is fundamental to the OCIA process. Using the *Revised Edition of New American Bible*, (NABRE), *The Word Into Life* offers commentary and questions for discussion to bring the Sunday Scriptures alive.

The Word Into Life can be used for Bible study groups, to aid in the preparation of homilies and to reinforce The *Journey of Faith* program, enhancing the OCIA process.

Catholic Update and More

Liguori Publications offers many resources for OCIA leaders and participants, including DVDs, pamphlets, and electronic publications. *Catholic Update* newsletters explore Catholic teaching and tradition in easy to understand language. Because they often address the sacraments and topics of interest to an adult OCIA audience, suggested *Catholic Update* newsletters are included in each lesson plan.

No matter how far in advance you plan your purchase, unexpected things come up. You know photocopying material is a violation of the copyright, but what do you do when you are pressed for time?

Liguori can help in these kinds of emergencies through rush delivery. Please call us at 1-800-325-9521 or email us at Liguori@Liguori.org to find out how we can help.

Breaking Open the Word, Years A, B, and C
An OCIA Guide to Sunday Scripture
MARY KATHARINE DEELEY
200-page paperback / 8.5 x 11
Year A 9780764-826627
Year B 9780764-827662
Year C 9780764-828171

The Word Into Life, Years A, B, and C
A Guide for Group Reflection on Sunday Scripture
A REDEMPTORIST PASTORAL PUBLICATION
176-page paperback / 8.5 x 11
Year A 9780764-816260
Year B 9780764-813498
Year C 9780764-815362

***Catholic Update* 100+ Set: Topics for OCIA**
A REDEMPTORIST PASTORAL PUBLICATION
Set of 100 / 8.5 x 11 / JF0013

Practical Suggestions

Materials and Supplies

The leader preparation tips suggest helpful items specific to each lesson. For most sessions, you will need the following:

- a complete set of *Journey of Faith* handouts for each participant (It's best to buy additional sets for sponsors.)
- copies of the *Journey of Faith Leader Guides* for each catechist and team member
- copies of *Breaking Open the Word* or *The Word Into Life* for each catechist and team member (optional but recommended)
- multiple, ideally individual, copies of the Holy Bible (*Journey of Faith* uses the *New American Bible,* revised edition.)
- multiple, ideally individual, copies of the *Catechism of the Catholic Church (CCC)*
- a Bible concordance to help leaders locate related passages (optional)
- a simple white candle in a secure holder
- matches or a lighter
- nametags for the first few sessions
- comfortable seating for each individual positioned near tables or other writing/working surfaces
- pens, pencils, and notebooks or paper (see Journaling and Notes sidebar)

Journaling and Notes

Like the faith journey, the reflection and writing process can be highly personal. Some write more than others or prefer certain mediums and styles. The handouts offer limited writing space for questions, Bible references, and activities. However, keeping an OCIA journal fulfills a number of purposes:

- recalling thoughts and reactions to the topics, readings, and discussions
- writing longer responses to the questions and activities
- jotting down notes and questions during and beyond the sessions
- recording insights, ideas, and feelings throughout the OCIA process

At the first session, provide all participants with a journal, or, if they prefer, they may bring their own. Encourage them to use it every week and to spend time in personal reflection. Let them know they are not required to share anything private with the group or with their sponsor.

Preparing a Sacred Space

Scripture reading, faith discussions, and prayer require reverence. Your environment sets the tone for each session and much of the process. Make sure the room has an inviting atmosphere. Modifying the space to match the session's topic, OCIA period, or liturgical season will assist the participants as they move through the process and grow in their familiarity with Catholic culture, ethos, and identity. You may also want to pray with the group for the Holy Spirit to be with you as you begin your opening Scripture each session to better prepare the hearts and minds of participants and yourself as a leader.

- Reverently lay the Bible or *Lectionary* next to the candle. During each of the sacred seasons, place liturgically colored fabric underneath: green during Ordinary Time, violet during Advent and Lent, and white during Christmas and Easter.
- Add religious images and objects to the space.
- Appeal to all of the participants' senses. Consider playing sacred music as they enter the space or meditative sounds as they pray or write in their journals. Encourage anyone who provides refreshments to be creative and to match the snack to the topic, season, or a saint whose feast lands on or near the session date.

In the Beginning: The First Few Sessions

1. Warmly welcome the participants, sponsors, and guests. Encourage sponsors to attend every session with their participant.

2. Have each person introduce himself or herself. Ask each one to briefly explain what led him or her to inquire about the Catholic faith or accept a supporting role in the OCIA. Encourage people to share information about their family and faith backgrounds.

3. Distribute the materials, state your expectations for the program, and give any instructions or announcements, such as directions to the restrooms.

4. Explain the purpose and meaning of the sessions. Uncatechized teens may not be familiar with prayer, candlelighting, Scripture reading and reflection, faith sharing, or religious instruction—especially in a Catholic setting.

5. Whenever reading from Scripture, make sure the reader is comfortable with reading aloud and understands the passage. Scripture should be proclaimed prayerfully and clearly and, if possible, with prior preparation. Never oblige anyone, but invite all interested to receive guidance from a practiced leader or minister.

6. Always model the behavior and etiquette desired, whether at Mass or in the sessions. While gentle reminders are needed at times, people of all ages learn from example.

7. Allow time before, after, or outside the sessions for fellowship, socializing, and refreshments. This allows the personal connections and private conversations essential to spiritual growth to take place.

Answering Questions

Most participants enter the OCIA process with religious or spiritual questions as well as preconceived notions of the Catholic Church. More questions will undoubtedly emerge as they near initiation. Furthermore, the time they spend in the sessions and even with the parish community will not completely encompass their experience and knowledge of faith. Catechists and team members must be willing to engage tough questions and events in order to further the individual's understanding and conversion.

Always respect every question and respond to it as adequately as you can, especially if it is pertinent to the topic and the entire group. Never attempt to answer a question that goes beyond your knowledge or expertise.

If you don't feel qualified or aren't sure how to answer:

- Let the person know you need time to prepare a proper or fuller answer. Offer to respond at the next session or outside of the sessions, and follow through.
- Check trusted and authoritative sources for relevant Church teachings and key factors in your response. Share your references or recommend similar material when the question is revisited.
- Consult with your director or coordinator of religious education, pastor, or diocesan official, or set up a private conversation between that contact and the person to answer the question more thoroughly.

If an individual query or a barrage of questions draw the discussion away from the topic at hand, consider dedicating a portion or an entire session to the subject of interest.

OCIA Schedules Using *Journey of Faith*

Program or Academic Year (Fall–Pentecost)

The following guidelines direct parishes in scheduling an OCIA program lasting eight to nine months each year. Weekly schedules may vary from year to year depending on when Advent, Lent, and the rites occur. Merging or separating lessons into adjacent weeks will keep you on track and maximize the program's connection to liturgical feasts and themes.

Journey of Faith strongly recommends continuing after Easter into a discrete period of mystagogy. This provides the parish an additional opportunity to join the neophytes and witness to the value of, and universal call to, ongoing faith formation.

Three Months Before Advent (August-September)		
First Week	Q1	"Welcome to the OCIA!"
Second Week	Q2	"What Is Faith?"
Third Week	Q3	"The Holy Trinity"
Fourth Week	Q4	"Who Is Jesus Christ?"

Two Months Before Advent (September-October)		
First Week	Q5	"The Bible"
	Q6	"Divine Revelation"
Second Week	Q7	"Your Prayer Life"
	Q8	"Catholic Prayers and Practices"
Third Week	Q9	"The Mass"
	C5	"The Sacrament of the Eucharist"
Fourth Week	Q10	"The Church Year"
	Q11	"Places in a Catholic Church"

One Month Before Advent (October-November)		
First Week	Q12	"Who Shepherds the Church?"
	Q13	"The Church as Community"
Second Week	Q14	"Mary"
	Q15	"The Saints"
Third Week	Q16	"Eschatology: The 'Last Things'"
Fourth Week/ Christ the King	C1	"The OCIA Process and Rites" (anticipates rites of acceptance and welcoming)

Advent and Christmas (November-December)		
First Week	C10	"The People of God"
Second Week	C11	"The Early Church"
	C12	"Church History"
Third Week	C2	"The Sacraments: An Introduction"
Fourth Week/ Christmas		BREAK
Holy Family/ Epiphany	C8	"The Sacrament of Matrimony"
	C9	"The Sacrament of Holy Orders"
Baptism of the Lord (OT)	C3	"The Sacrament of Baptism"
	C4	"The Sacrament of Confirmation"

One Month Before Lent (January-February)		
First Week	C6	"The Sacrament of Penance and Reconciliation"
	C7	"The Sacrament of Anointing of the Sick"
Second Week	C13	"Christian Moral Living"
	C14	"The Dignity of Life"
Third Week	C15	"A Consistent Ethic of Life"
	C16	"Social Justice"
Week of Ash Wednesday	E1	"Election: Saying 'Yes' to Jesus (anticipates rite of election)"

Lent/Enlightenment (February-March)		
First Week	E2	"Living Lent"
Second Week	E3	"Scrutinizes: Looking Within"
	E4	"The Creed" (anticipates third Sunday)
Third Week	E5	"The Way of the Cross"
Fourth Week	E6	"The Lord's Prayer" (anticipates fifth Sunday)
Fifth Week	E7	"The Meaning of Holy Week"
Holy Week	E8	Easter Vigil Retreat

Easter/Mystagogy (April-May)		
First Week		BREAK (or appropriate fellowship)
Second Week	M1	"Conversion: A Lifelong Process"
Third Week	M2	"The Role of the Laity";
	M7	"Family Life"
Fourth Week	M3	"Your Spiritual Gifts"
Fifth Week	M4	"Discernment"
Sixth Week/ Ascension	M5	"Our Call to Holiness"
	M6	"Living the Virtues"
Seventh Week/ Pentecost (Final Session)	M8	"Evangelization"

Calendar Year (ongoing, sequential)

The forty-eight *Journey of Faith* lessons can be followed sequentially with only minor adjustments for the rites and the Lenten season. Using this model, parishes would begin about *four weeks after Pentecost*. To complete the calendar year, we recommend a single-week break for Christmas and Easter and a two-week break shortly after Pentecost for program renewal, training, and family time. Refer to the *Journey of Faith* lessons listed in My OCIA Schedule.

Liturgical Year (ongoing, nonsequential)

For parishes following the ongoing catechumenal model, each period in the OCIA process is available all year long. We recommend using separate but simultaneous tracks for inquiry and catechumenate and a third track during Lent and Easter. In this way, the process is open and flexible enough to support and honor the needs and pace of each catechumen and candidate.

In this model, most individuals will spend a year or more in the OCIA process. The lessons will be used as they relate to the themes of each Sunday's readings. All forty-eight lessons are applied within each volume of *The Word Into Life*, so no matter when you start, a year-long formation will nearly guarantee a complete exploration of the topics in the program. Any gaps can be incorporated into the individual's process if time is a factor and doing so is prudent.

My OCIA Schedule

This chart can be reused or adjusted each year according to your parish's OCIA calendar. It is also valuable for participants who may be on a separate path from the rest of the group. Make sure to record all key dates and details and to follow your OCIA director's or pastor's instructions.

Parish: ____________________

Pastor/ OCIA Director: ____________________

Catechist(s)/ Team Member(s): ____________________

Participant(s): ____________________

Class Time(s): ____________________

Class Location: ____________________

Mass Time: ____________________

Easter Vigil: ____________________

INQUIRY			
Lesson Title	**Session Date**	**Lesson Title**	**Session Date**
Q1: Welcome to the OCIA		Q9: The Mass	
Q2: What Is Faith?		Q10: The Church Year	
Q3: The Holy Trinity		Q11: Places in a Catholic Church	
Q4: Who Is Jesus Christ?		Q12: Who Shepherds the Church?	
Q5: The Bible		Q13: The Church as Community	
Q6: Divine Revelation		Q14: Mary	
Q7: Your Prayer Life		Q15: The Saints	
Q8: Catholic Prayers and Practices		Q16: Eschatology: the "Last Things"	

CATECHUMENATE			
Lesson Title	**Session Date**	**Lesson Title**	**Session Date**
C1: The OCIA Process and Rites		C9: The Sacrament of Holy Orders	
C2: The Sacraments: An Introduction		C10: The People of God	
C3: The Sacrament of Baptism		C11: The Early Church	
C4: The Sacrament of Confirmation		C12: Church History	
C5: The Sacrament of the Eucharist		C13: Christian Moral Living	
C6: The Sacrament of Penance and Reconciliation		C14: The Dignity of Life	
C7: The Sacrament of Anointing of the Sick		C15: A Consistent Ethic of Life	
C8: The Sacrament of Matrimony		C16: Social Justice	

Enlightenment		Mystagogy	
Lesson Title	**Session Date**	**Lesson Title**	**Session Date**
E1: Election: Saying "Yes" to Jesus		M1: Conversion: A Lifelong Process	
E2: Living Lent		M2: The Role of the Laity	
E3: Scrutinies: Looking Within		M3: Your Spiritual Gifts	
E4: The Creed		M4: Discernment	
E5: The Way of the Cross		M5: Our Call to Holiness	
E6: The Lord's Prayer		M6: Living the Virtues	
E7: The Meaning of Holy Week		M7: Family Life	
E8: Easter Vigil Retreat		M8: Evangelization	

Q1: Welcome to the OCIA

Catechism: 1229–1249

Objectives

- Identify the OCIA as a time to ask questions about the Catholic faith.
- Differentiate between the four periods of the OCIA process.
- Describe the origins of the OCIA.
- Engage in thoughtful spiritual reflection.

Leader Meditation

Psalm 139:1–16

Think about your own faith journey. Consider the many times God has protected and guided you. Now, consider the ones this same God is guiding and entrusting to your care. Imagine the trust God has in you. You have been given the opportunity to be their companion and guide on their faith journey. Pray for wisdom and courage. Rely on the Lord's help.

Leader Preparation

- Read the lesson handout, this lesson plan, the Scripture passage, and *Catechism* sections.
- Read the front sections of this Leader Guide. The USCCB website may also help you explain the OCIA and *Catechism* further.
- Gather copies of the *New American Bible* and *Catechism* for each participant as well as any required materials listed earlier in this guide under "Materials and Supplies." Enlist creative ways to supply prayer journals and other unique items (see "Integrating the Parish Community").
- Be familiar with the vocabulary terms for this lesson: OCIA, catechist, catechumenate, godparent, sponsor, sacraments of initiation, mystagogy, scrutinies, catechism. Definitions can be found in this guide's glossary.

Welcome

As participants arrive, welcome each individual, repeating back each name. Direct participants to the supplies, nametags, refreshments, and restrooms. Take time for group introductions. After giving initial instructions and announcements, take questions and respond briefly. Begin promptly.

Opening Scripture

Psalm 139:1–16

If any inquirer is unfamiliar with the Bible, briefly review its organization and how to look up readings before you begin. Light the candle and explain that it is a sign and a reminder of the Lord's presence.

Ask for a volunteer to read aloud. Afterward, allow a moment of silence, and then welcome reactions to the words. Share a few words of encouragement and affirmation. Let the participants know that God is leading them and has been with them from the beginning. Before you go into the discussion of the lesson, ask participants to ***think about all the things that happened to bring them here to the OCIA.***

> God...reveals himself and gives himself to man, at the same time bringing man a superabundant light as he searches for the ultimate meaning of his life.
>
> CCC 153

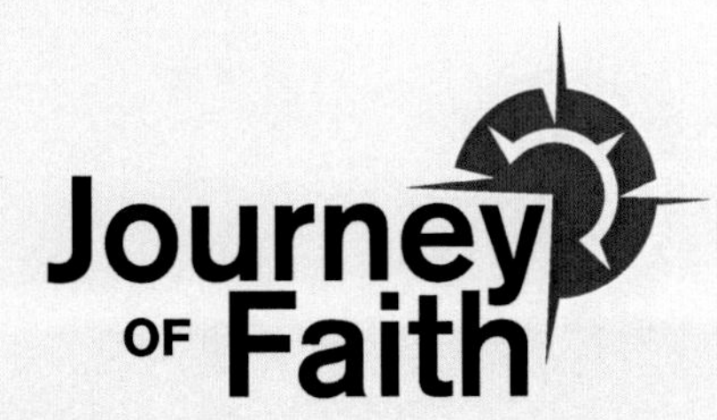

INQUIRY Q1

In Short:

- The OCIA is a time to ask faith questions.
- The OCIA has four periods.
- The OCIA is rooted in early Christian history.

Welcome to the OCIA

So today you start the OCIA. (See the bottom of the last page to find out why the name was changed from RCIA to OCIA). Maybe you're here because you feel called to the Catholic Church. Maybe your whole family is going through the OCIA process. Maybe your parents want you to receive the sacraments of Eucharist or confirmation. All of these are good reasons. Maybe you're having a hard time seeing how any of this is good for you right now. That's OK, too.

- Think about a time when you heard about a great new movie. Maybe friends told you or you heard through social media that this was the must-see movie of the year. You trust the reviews and make plans to go see it. But once the movie starts, you realize it takes a while for that great story to happen. You have to sit through every scene in order to see the really good parts. Great events often take time. Sometimes we have to be patient before we get to the good part!

Jesus knows how much we want to enjoy life, so he offers an authentic path to lasting happiness for people of every age and culture. Making it down that path takes time. Lasting happiness is what the OCIA is all about, so it's worth planning to attend the OCIA sessions. Through the OCIA, you will come to understand the way of Jesus Christ and have a chance to ask any question you have about religion, such as:

- Does God really exist? Why do I exist?
- Who is Jesus? Is he the only way to salvation?
- What is the Catholic Church and why should I join it?

Take Your Time!

Courses in school and college should be decided upon slowly. Making lasting friendships takes even more time. Spending time with friends means sharing experiences, dreams, fears, and heartbreaks. You begin a kind of journey with friends where you continue to grow, understand, and trust each other. It's the same with Jesus.

Catholics believe our faith is not so much a set of beliefs (although we certainly have them!) but more a relationship that we start, develop, and continue to grow in with our Lord.

Thoughtful Reflection Is Good!

Feelings can be powerful and wonderful, but you wouldn't want a friendship that comes *only* from a sudden rush of feeling. Friendships are stronger when they evolve from well-considered, *free* choices from everyone involved. These are the relationships that are solid and lasting.

- *How do you normally make really big decisions?*
- *How did you decide to start the OCIA?*

TEENS

© 2023 Liguori Publications. Photocopying prohibited

CCC 1229–1233, 1247–1249

Welcome to the OCIA

- For today's lesson, start with the activity at the end of the participant handout *(see "Activity" section of this lesson plan for instructions)*. This will help the group get to know each other and enable participants to open up and participate in a low-pressure way as you get started.
- Give participants a short overview of what will happen in their OCIA classes. You'll explain each period in more detail later, so keep your overview informal and focused on what participants can expect each time they meet.
- Encourage participants to keep a spiritual or prayer journal during their time in the OCIA. Emphasize that it can be used not only for reflection questions in class but for any thoughts or questions about faith they have on their own.
- Introduce participants to the *Catechism*. Explain how to use it and emphasize it doesn't need to be read cover to cover.
- Ask participants to share what brought them to the OCIA. *Share what brought you to the OCIA as a leader, too.*

Why Do We Have an OCIA Program?

- Discuss some Catholics you admire and why. Encourage participants to share their own responses. *These can be saints, holy people, or people from your life.*

Is This a New Process?

- Review the history and purpose of the OCIA. Emphaszie that participants do not need to become experts in doctrine or prayer. Rather, they will receive instruction on basic teachings and beliefs and guided practice in various spiritual activities, including the rites.

Jesus doesn't just ask us to follow him into the faith blindly. He wants us to make the choice freely and with all the information we need to make a decision. We can see examples of this in Scripture:

> *"Come, and you will see!"*
>
> John 1:39

Jesus invites people to observe him closely over time to see if he accomplishes what he says he will. We will observe Jesus closely during these OCIA sessions.

> *"Come after me."*
>
> Matthew 4:19

These three words are the simplest definition of our faith. In fact, they are the first words Jesus spoke when he began his ministry. Notice he didn't say, *"Understand me"* or even, *"Believe in me."* He simply asked people to observe him closely and then freely choose on their own to follow in his footsteps.

Why Do We Have an OCIA Program?

Jesus asked those first Christians to "go, therefore, and make disciples of all nations…" (Matthew 28:19). Christians made disciples because they believed that following Jesus would make others happier and more at peace. We believe the Catholic understanding of Jesus' teachings is the fullest and most authentic understanding of Jesus. Your OCIA classes will be led by a **catechist**, someone who teaches the principles of the Christian religion to others.

> *"I came so that they might have life and have it more abundantly."*
>
> John 10:10

> *"I have told you this so that my joy may be in you and your joy may be complete."*
>
> John 15:11

- *Who are some Catholics you admire? What do you admire about them?*
- *What do you think about the early Christians' mission to make disciples?*

What Does the OCIA Mean?

The letters stand for **Order of Christian Initiation of Adults**. It is the learning program for people to become *initiated* or *enter* the Catholic Church. It also includes *rites*, or rituals, usually done at Sunday Mass (see lesson C1).

Its main purpose is to help those who are interested in becoming Catholic do so or to help those who want to receive **sacraments** like Communion or confirmation that they missed earlier in life but would like to receive now. (More on the sacraments in later lessons.)

Is This a New Process?

This learning program began in the earliest years of the Church. Christians then knew it was hard to convert to Christianity because the Roman Empire persecuted Christians. The Church wanted to make sure that candidates really knew what they were getting into and that they were willing to stand up for their faith in a sometimes hostile pagan environment. In the mid-twentieth century, the Church decided to return to this process by offering solid Christian education in the same gradual manner that people enter any lasting and loving relationship.

What Happens in the OCIA?

Most OCIA programs involve a series of weekly sessions with a team of teachers, sponsors, and fellow candidates.

Each session is a safe place for you to hear about our faith and to ask questions about Catholicism or faith in general. If the team leaders do not know the answer to a question, they will research it and get back to you with a response. All questions are welcomed and honored.

Go Ahead and Ask: *Mary questions God when she's told she's going to be the mother of Jesus (Luke 1:34). God answers because Jesus could not be born without her free and informed consent. That is how much God respects and even expects your honest questions.*

Why Does Jesus Ask Me to Join a Church Community?

Jesus knows we are deeply affected by the behavior of others and wants our behavior to positively affect others' behavior as well. That happens in the community we call the Church.

Faith and love are both private *and* public behaviors. When others see you visibly express your friendship, it can inspire them to become better friends. Friendship is powerful! So is our faith. At those Sundays when the rest of the parish sees you at the OCIA rites, it can inspire them to live their faith better as well.

Wouldn't you rather know?
It is hard to see ourselves clearly. We need someone else to see what we cannot see ourselves, like a friend telling us we still have food stuck in our teeth, or a coach showing us how to make free throws, or a wise mentor on how to improve our work. We don't mind someone coaching us if it helps us improve!

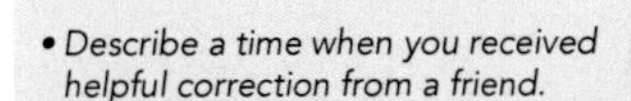

- *Describe a time when you received helpful correction from a friend.*

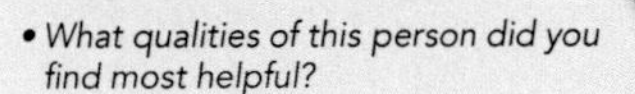

- *What qualities of this person did you find most helpful?*

Periods of the OCIA

Inquiry
This title simply describes the attitude and behavior of people like you right now. You are just inquiring or testing the waters and asking questions. You're not asked to make any commitments or promises. This stage may last for a few months.

Catechumenate
This word is from ancient Greek and means "student." It begins with a rite of acceptance in which you simply promise to be a good student. During this stage you will study and discuss most of the main beliefs of our faith and choose a **godparent** or **sponsor** to join you on your journey. A sponsor can be a wise friend or relative or someone suggested by the team. They join you each week and even between sessions for more discussion.

Purification and Enlightenment *(Lent)*
This stage is in the final weeks before Easter and is more prayerful than instructional. It is a time of deeper spiritual preparation for the sacraments you will receive at Easter. The name affirms that God has *elected* or *chosen* you to follow him. It includes the *rite of sending,* where your parish church prayerfully sends you as a group to attend Mass with the local bishop for a special blessing. There are also three additional rites called **scrutinies** that ask God to help your self-examination or self-scrutiny where you seek to increase what is good and decrease what does not belong in your spiritual life. You receive the **sacraments of initiation** at Holy Saturday Mass, the Easter Vigil. Those who have been preparing all this time finally enter the Church and receive the sacraments of baptism, confirmation, and Eucharist.

Mystagogy
This is the final stage and lasts a few more weeks. It's a time to reflect on how you can practically put the sacraments you have just received into effect. *Mystagogia* is a Greek word meaning "to learn the mysteries we have received."

- *What are your thoughts and feelings about the rites of the OCIA?*

How Should I Attend Meetings?

Show up—*Really* show up!

Be openhearted: Come with an eagerness to learn.

Ask questions: Help resolve whatever your concerns or questions are.

Talk to wise mentors: Understanding grows when you discuss ideas with trusted friends.

Pray for wisdom: Ask Jesus himself for what you need to follow him.

Read the *Catechism of the Catholic Church (CCC)*: A **catechism** is a summary of religious teachings for the purpose of instruction.

This book will be a great asset for your journey!

Why Does Jesus Ask Me to Join a Church Community

- Ask participants why faith can be strengthened by a Church community.

Suggested responses include: we can be a positive influence to others, we receive support in times of struggle, we can make friends, we are accountable to others, and we can go somewhere with our questions.

- Ask participants to share their thoughts on the early Christians' mission to make disciples.

Periods of the OCIA

- Discuss the elements of each period of the OCIA. Ask participants if they have any questions about any of the periods.

Write three facts about yourself on separate sheets of paper. Place the sheets in a pile. Your leader will mix them up. Take turns drawing one at random and guess who it belongs to.

JOURNEY OF FAITH **INQUIRY**

Take time to get to know the other people in your class.

Write three facts about yourself on separate sheets of paper. Place the sheets in a pile. Your leader will mix them up. Take turns drawing one at random and guess who it belongs to.

While most are eager to begin the OCIA, they might still have many questions and even some reservations.

What questions do you have as you start the OCIA?

What concerns, reservations, or hesitations do you have?

Journey of Faith for Teens: Inquiry, Q1 (826337)

The process by which adults are initiated into the Catholic faith throughout the United States is now called the OCIA—the Order of Christian Initiation of Adults. "Order" is a clearer translation of the Latin term for the process formerly known as the RCIA—the Rite of Christian Initiation of Adults. People preparing for baptism and reception into the Church celebrate several rites as part of the order to which those rites belong—an order whose mission is to journey in the faith. The US Conference of Catholic Bishops adopted the name change in 2021, with American dioceses introducing the name thereafter. For more information, please contact your local diocese.

Imprimi Potest: Stephen T. Rehrauer, CSsR, Provincial, Denver Province, the Redemptorists.

Imprimatur: "In accordance with CIC 827, permission to publish has been granted on March 29, 2016, by the Most Reverend Edward M. Rice, Auxiliary Bishop, Archdiocese of St. Louis. Permission to publish is an indication that nothing contrary to Church teaching is contained in this work. It does not imply any endorsement of the opinions expressed in the publication; nor is any liability assumed by this permission."

Journey of Faith for Teens © 2000, 2016 Liguori Publications, Liguori, MO 63057. All rights reserved. No part of this publication may be reproduced, distributed, stored, transmitted, or posted in any form by any means without prior written permission. To order, visit Liguori.org or call 800-325-9521. Liguori Publications, a nonprofit corporation, is an apostolate of the Redemptorists. To learn more about the Redemptorists, visit Redemptorists.com.

© 2023 Liguori Publications. Photocopying prohibited

Contributing writer: Fr. Dave Heney. Editors of 2016 edition: Theresa Nienaber and Pat Fosarelli, MD, DMin. Design: Lorena Mitre Jimenez. Images: Shutterstock.

Scripture texts in this work are taken from the *New American Bible*, revised edition ©2010, 1991, 1986, 1970 Confraternity of Christian Doctrine, Washington, D.C., and are used by permission of the copyright owner. All Rights Reserved. No part of the New American Bible may be reproduced in any form without permission in writing from the copyright owner. Excerpts from English translation of the *Catechism of the Catholic Church* for the United States of America © 1994 United States Catholic Conference, Inc. —*Libreria Editrice Vaticana*; English translation of the Catechism of the Catholic Church: Modifications from the Editio Typica © 1997 United States Catholic Conference, Inc. —*Libreria Editrice Vaticana*. Compliant with *The Roman Missal, Third Edition*.

Printed in the United States of America.
Third Edition.

Liguori PUBLICATIONS
A Redemptorist Ministry

ISBN 978-0-7648-2633-7
9 780764 826337 90000>

Journaling

While most people are eager to begin the OCIA, they might still have many questions and even some reservations. What questions do you have as you start the OCIA? What concerns or hesitations do you have?

Closing Prayer

Close with a simple prayer.

Jesus, Lord of Life, you are the true shepherd. You care for us as a shepherd cares for his sheep. Continue to lead us up and down the paths of life and guide us to safety. You defend us with your life, and we are beginning to recognize your voice. Amen.

Looking Ahead

Before the next session, have participants spend time thinking about their own faith journey so far. Ask them: "How'd you get here from where you started? What did you take with you? What did you have to leave behind?"

Q2: What Is Faith

Catechism: 142–165, 302, 854

Objectives

Participants will…

- Understand faith is given freely by God and helps us understand God's love.
- Realize that having faith does not mean ignoring science or rational thought.
- Recognize that for faith to grow it must be practiced both alone and in community.

Leader Meditation

John 14:1–4

Read the Scripture passage, then think about the strength of your own faith. When you pray, do you believe your prayers are being heard? Do you trust that God is intimately involved in your life, even with all its difficulties and imperfections? Most important, do you see the face of God in the questioning, doubting, and sometimes challenging young people you teach?

Leader Preparation

- Read the lesson, this lesson plan, the Scripture passage, and the *Catechism* sections. "The Characteristics of Faith" (*CCC* 153–165) may help you to answer questions posed by your class, especially how faith relates to science.
- Be familiar with the vocabulary term for this lesson: faith. The definition can be found in this guide's glossary.

Welcome

As participants arrive, welcome any new inquirers and sponsors. Check for supplies and immediate needs. Ask for any questions or comments about last week's lesson that may have come up during the week. Begin promptly.

Opening Scripture

John 14:1–4

Ask a volunteer to light the candle and read aloud.

Following the reading, allow a moment of silence, and then welcome any comments or reactions to the words.

Finally, ask for any special intentions. Before beginning the discussion of the lesson handout, ask participants, ***"How easy is it for you to 'take things on faith?'"*** Allow time for responses.

Faith is a gift of God, a supernatural virtue infused by [God].

CCC 153

INQUIRY Q2

In Short:

- Faith is a virtue freely given by God.
- Faith, science, and reason coexist.
- Faith grows when we're alone and part of a community.

What Is Faith?

Some people love to get lost in an adventure. Their journeys can last years and cover miles. They thrive on not knowing what will come next, who they'll meet, or where they'll end up. They don't care if they head off into their journey unprepared—planning lessens the adventure.

Other people aren't quite as ready to leave everything to chance. They make plans, figure out what they need to pack, and trace exactly where they'll go. They don't leave room for the uncertain—they don't have room on their adventure for the unexpected.

- *Do you think either of these ways is the best way to travel? Why or why not?*
- *What's the purpose of going on a journey?*
- *What kind of journey has your own life been?*

Life is a process. A journey is a process, too. Both involve growth, change, and development. When we're on a journey, we don't stay in the same place, at least not for long. We move on. We choose new roads. We discover new things. We grow in wisdom and understanding. We mature. We are always in process.

The Journey of Faith

Faith means having certainty in God and all his works and is more certain than all human knowledge. However, having faith doesn't mean never asking questions or ignoring empirical facts. Actually, as your faith grows, so does your desire to know more about God. Faith is a grace we can't have without God, but it's also a human act. So while God can give us the grace and courage to live and act with faith, it's still up to us to take those steps (CCC 156–162). When we have faith, we live each moment knowing that God loves us, even when life seems to tell us otherwise. To have faith means to trust that nothing, absolutely nothing, can separate us from the love of God.

Faith is also a process. It's the most important process and most important journey of our lives because it brings us closer to God. The more we live our faith, the closer we get to God. Being close to God brings us an inner joy and peace that can't come from anything else. We all want to feel close to God, yet the process of getting there may seem difficult, if not impossible.

Let's take a deeper look at what it means to have faith in God.

> *"What will separate us from the love of Christ? Will anguish, or distress, or persecution, or famine, or nakedness, or peril, or the sword?...No, in all these things we conquer overwhelmingly through him who loved us."*
>
> Romans 8:35, 37

TEENS

© 2023 Liguori Publications. Photocopying prohibited

CCC 142–165, 302, 854

The Journey of Faith

- Discuss what the process of faith entails.

Suggested responses may include: asking questions, desiring to know more about God, taking steps to live like Jesus, trusting that God loves us, and more.

- Emphasize that this process never ends, faith is always growing, and we will never be finished with our faith formation on earth.
- As you go over the reflection questions for this section, also discuss how faith in God is different from, or similar to, having faith in people or things.

Ask participants to pick one of the following passages with a partner, group, or on their own and share what they learned about faith. You may need to direct them to a particular page number until you cover lesson Q5 *The Bible*.

- Mark 9:23
everything is possible when you have faith in God

- Matthew 21:22
whatever you ask for in prayer, you will receive

Remind participants that God answers our prayers in his own time and often in ways we don't expect. So while God does answer all our prayers, he may not give us exactly what we want.

- 1 Peter 1:8–9
because we have faith we will experience salvation

Remind participants that having faith isn't passive. We must live out our faith actively, not just claim it in words only.

Our Personal Faith

Have participants answer the reflection question on their own, or if you have time do the following activity as a group. Make a list of circumstances that might make us doubt God or our faith. Then make a list of ways we can use our faith to help us in those scenarios.

Suggested responses include: After the death of a loved one we can reach out to a priest, youth minister, or other spiritual guide with questions or frustrations. We can read Scripture passages about life after death, or talk to our loved one in prayer.

After the end of a relationship or friendship we can share our doubts, concerns, or frustrations with God in prayer. We can seek forgiveness for anything we did wrong from both the other person involved and God (through prayer or, in a special way, the sacrament of reconciliation).

INQUIRY

JOURNEY OF FAITH

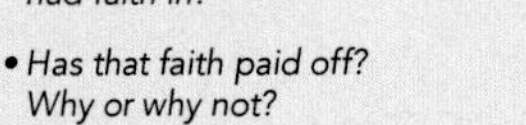

- *What are some other things you've had faith in?*
- *Has that faith paid off? Why or why not?*

The teachings of the Catholic Church on faith come largely from Scripture.

Take a few moments and look up the following passages in your Bible. Then briefly write or discuss what each passage means:

Mark 9:23 Matthew 21:22

1 Peter 1:8–9

Our Personal Faith

Because faith involves trust in something that goes beyond our human understanding, it can be very difficult to accept. As a teen, you're transitioning into the adult you will become. That's a process filled with questions and doubts, a time when you question nearly everything you once believed to be true. You'll question your parents and society—their wisdom, their values, and their beliefs. You might even find yourself looking around and wondering, "Isn't there anyone else I can ask?"

It can be tempting to trade in these questions for answers, to want these mysteries of faith to be solved. You might think that having faith means you're no longer allowed to ask questions or that you have to give up your own opinions to blindly follow some Church authority. Rest assured, having faith doesn't mean we stop asking questions; it means we live like we are loved and desired by God—and that we treat others like they are, too.

When we become people of faith, we take on the values of Jesus Christ. But while living like Jesus leads us to a more authentic life, it isn't an easy lifestyle. It can seem like the world values beautiful people and expensive things over values like simple living, chastity, and sacrifice.

The good news is, you're not alone. There are a lot of people of faith out there, and they're struggling to live like Jesus, too. If you're able to tune out noise from the rest of the world, you'll see you're not in this alone.

- *Are there circumstances where you find it difficult to live your faith? How do you handle them?*

Sometimes even when we do have faith, we don't always feel sure of our beliefs. We shouldn't judge our closeness to God by how we feel. God is just as close to us when we're depressed, irritated, or stressed out as when we're joyful and carefree. When we're going through tough times, we can feel like God is very far away. But God's perfect love for us is always there, even in times of doubt and trouble. We cannot hide from the love of our Lord.

When we question God, we may not receive the answers we want. But that doesn't mean God isn't listening or that he doesn't care about us. God reaches out to us in our ordinary, everyday lives. God wants us to become the thinking, creative, feeling people we were created to be, and sometimes that means struggling with our faith or changing part of how we live.

In the future, when you start to worry about this thing, pray: *"I give the burden to God, I relax and let go."* Then take a deep breath and as you breathe out, know that God is taking your burden and working on it.

- *How do you handle times of fear, mistrust, or a lack of faith?*
- *Think of something that you're trying very hard to control in your life. Perhaps you struggle with a particular classmate, school subject, or family member. It could be a person, a situation, anything. Write it down.*
- *What about that situation can you give up and turn over to God?*

Q2

Q2

INQUIRY

JOURNEY OF FAITH

Called to Faith

"Now Saul, still breathing murderous threats against the disciples of the Lord, went to the high priest and asked him for letters to the synagogues in Damascus, that, if he should find any men or women who belonged to the Way, he might bring them back to Jerusalem in chains."

Acts 9:1–2

For some, the gift of faith comes in surprising ways. One day, a man named Saul was making a journey to the town of Damascus. All of a sudden he was blinded by a flash of light and heard a voice from heaven. "He fell to the ground and heard a voice saying to him, 'Saul, Saul, why are you persecuting me?'" (Acts 9:4). He went from someone who persecuted Christians to a follower of Jesus Christ himself and a great teacher, spreading the story of Jesus throughout his part of the world. God even changed Saul's name to Paul as a sign of his new identity as a follower of Jesus (Acts 9:1–19).

For most of us, our faith beginning isn't as dramatic. God is like a quiet gardener who knows where the "good soil" lies within us better than we do. God plants the first small seed. But if we want our faith to grow, we have to be active about it. Once you ask God for the gift of faith, God gives it to you freely. But we can't just ask God to give us the gift of faith and be done with it. We have to nurture the faith he gives us. We can't expect our faith in God to grow if we do nothing.

There's another important element in Paul's story, too. Once he found faith, he didn't keep it a secret. He went out and told other people about Jesus. He spread his faith to others. You might not be called to be a missionary or an evangelist like Paul, but you are called to share your faith in some way. And the more you share your faith, the stronger it will grow.

- *What have you learned about your faith so far that you are most excited to share with others?*

?

Growing Our Faith

Here are some things you can do to nurture your faith:

Read
Reading Scripture (the Bible) and other spiritual writings introduces you to the great wisdom of others. Spiritual reading gives you the knowledge and strength to resist the temptation to put other things before God—like money, power, popularity, physical beauty, or drugs.

Pray
For faith to grow, you must pray on your own and with others. If we want to get to know God, we must spend time talking with God. This means making time for quiet moments. Finding time to pray is sometimes the most difficult aspect of prayer.

Live
This is another challenging part of growing in faith. If you want to live authentically, the way you live your life must match your religious ideals. You may have friends who pressure you to do things that make you feel uncomfortable or that you know are wrong. Having faith means avoiding behaviors that would lead you away from God.

Get Involved
The Catholic sacraments of baptism, confirmation, and Eucharist will bring you into the life of the Church, the community of believers. As you live, work, and play with others, you come to know God, and you bring God to others. We belong to our community, and belonging helps our faith grow.

Q2

Called to Faith

If time allows, read the full account of Saul's conversion in the Bible (Acts 9:1–19).

Discuss why God might have chosen to speak to Saul and urge his conversion.

Ask participants what about Saul's story stands out the most to them and why.

Discuss the ways God plants seeds of faith in us.

Suggested responses include: putting inspirational people in our path, reading a relevant Scripture passage at the right time, and so forth.

Ask participants what they are most excited to share about their faith. Share what excites you most about your faith, too.

Growing Our Faith

After reading this section, brainstorm other ways participants might be able to grow their faith or opportunities in the four listed categories that are specific to your parish. *(If you have a parish youth group, youth choir, or special youth Mass let your participants know about it and when and where it meets.)*

Ask participants to share any questions about the faith, or common arguments they hear against the faith. Try to answer those questions as a group. *(If there are questions you can't answer, try to find answers for the next class.)*

With a group or as a class, imagine your journey of faith is a real journey. What would you need to pack? What would you have to leave behind? What obstacles might you face? What places or people might you see along the way?

Encourage participants to be creative here. They could draw pictures, create a comic, write a short story....They don't just have to write a list—although that's fine, too! You can also create a bag of your own to show as an example that includes a Bible, journal, prayer book, religious statue, and so on.

INQUIRY

JOURNEY OF FAITH

With a group or as a class, imagine your journey of faith is a real journey. What would you need to pack? What would you have to leave behind? What obstacles might you face? What places or people might you see along the way? You may write your responses in a list, draw scenes from the journey, or anything else you can think of to create.

What doubts do you have about your faith? Are there questions you still haven't answered or things you're still struggling to accept on faith? List them in your journal.

Find someone you're comfortable talking to and discuss these questions with that person.

Journey of Faith for Teens: Inquiry, Q2 (826337)

The process by which adults are initiated into the Catholic faith throughout the United States is now called the OCIA—the Order of Christian Initiation of Adults. "Order" is a clearer translation of the Latin term for the process formerly known as the RCIA—the Rite of Christian Initiation of Adults. People preparing for baptism and reception into the Church celebrate several rites as part of the order to which those rites belong—an order whose mission is to journey in the faith. The US Conference of Catholic Bishops adopted the name change in 2021, with American dioceses introducing the name thereafter. For more information, please contact your local diocese.

Imprimi Potest: Stephen T. Rehrauer, CSsR, Provincial, Denver Province, the Redemptorists.

Imprimatur: "In accordance with CIC 827, permission to publish has been granted on March 29, 2016, by the Most Reverend Edward M. Rice, Auxiliary Bishop, Archdiocese of St. Louis. Permission to publish is an indication that nothing contrary to Church teaching is contained in this work. It does not imply any endorsement of the opinions expressed in the publication; nor is any liability assumed by this permission."

Journey of Faith for Teens © 2000, 2016 Liguori Publications, Liguori, MO 63057. All rights reserved. No part of this publication may be reproduced, distributed, stored, transmitted, or posted in any form by any means without prior written permission.

© 2023 Liguori Publications. Photocopying prohibited

Contributing writer: Fr. Dave Heney. Editors of 2016 edition: Theresa Nienaber and Pat Fosarelli, MD, DMin. Design: Lorena Mitre Jimenez. Images: Shutterstock.

Scripture texts in this work are taken from the *New American Bible*, revised edition ©2010, 1991, 1986, 1970 Confraternity of Christian Doctrine, Washington, D.C., and are used by permission of the copyright owner. All Rights Reserved. No part of the New American Bible may be reproduced in any form without permission in writing from the copyright owner. Excerpts from English translation of the *Catechism of the Catholic Church* for the United States of America © 1994 United States Catholic Conference, Inc. —*Libreria Editrice Vaticana*; English translation of the Catechism of the Catholic Church: Modifications from the Editio Typica © 1997 United States Catholic Conference, Inc. —*Libreria Editrice Vaticana*. Compliant with *The Roman Missal, Third Edition*.

Printed in the United States of America. Third Edition.

To order, visit Liguori.org or call 800-325-9521. Liguori Publications, a nonprofit corporation, is an apostolate of the Redemptorists. To learn more about the Redemptorists, visit Redemptorists.com.

Liguori PUBLICATIONS A Redemptorist Ministry

Journey of Faith

Journaling

What doubts do you have about your faith? Are there questions you still haven't answered or things you're still struggling to accept on faith? List them in your journal. Find someone you're comfortable talking to and discuss these questions with that person.

Closing Prayer

Read aloud *The Prayer of a Seeker:*

Dear God, I'm walking this road without a map in my hand. Once I knew where I was headed on this journey, but now, I'm not so sure. Anyway, all I've got are a few directions scribbled down, some advice on how to read the road signs, maybe a place up ahead to ask the way when I get lost. Help me set my feet toward you. Steer me to those who will guide me wisely. Send me true companions along the road. Teach me that feeling lost may not be cause for panic but may lead to new and challenging paths. Let me know that you are always walking with me. Amen.

Looking Ahead

For next week, have participants think about faith as understanding God's love and how that might apply to the idea of the Trinity (God as the Father, the Son, and the Holy Spirit). Ask participants to think this week about their relationships with each member of the Trinity.

Q3: The Holy Trinity

Catechism: 232–267, 683–690

Objectives

- Explain the Trinity as an eternal communion of three divine persons: Father, Son, and Spirit.
- Cite examples of the Trinity revealed in Scripture and in the life of the Church.
- Define substance, person, and relation as used to discuss the Trinity.
- Assess their own relationship with the Trinity, focusing on the person they most overlook.

Leader Meditation

Matthew 3:16–17

Think about your relationship with the Blessed Trinity. When you pray, do you tend to pray to God the Father, God the Son, or God the Holy Spirit? Spend time in prayer now for a deeper relationship with the person you seem to most overlook.

Leader Preparation

- Read the lesson, this lesson plan, the Scripture passage, and the *Catechism* sections. These sections will be helpful in responding to the questions of participants from all faith backgrounds or participants with no faith background.
- Be familiar with vocabulary terms for this lesson: Trinity, substance, person, relation. Definitions are in this guide's glossary.
- Provide copies of the Nicene Creed for participants to refer to, in this session and beyond, as a summary of Catholic belief.
- Provide copies of a few prayers directed to each person of the Trinity. Demonstrating both ancient and new, formal and casual, adds variety and deepens the group's sense of each person's identity. *Some suggestions include the Glory Be, the Sign of the Cross, Act of Consecration to the Blessed Trinity, In Praise of the Trinity from The Roman Missal, and St. Augustine's Prayer for Zeal.*

Welcome

As participants arrive, welcome any new inquirers and sponsors. Check for supplies and immediate needs. Ask for questions or comments about last week's lesson that may have come up during the week. Begin promptly.

Opening Scripture

Matthew 3:16–17

Ask a volunteer to light the candle and read aloud. Afterward, allow a moment of silence and then welcome comments or reactions to the words. Before beginning your discussion of the lesson handout, ask participants, ***"What does this reading tell you about the persons of the Trinity?"***

> The mystery of the Most Holy Trinity is the central mystery of Christian faith and life. It is the mystery of God in himself. It is therefore the source of all the other mysteries of faith, the light that enlightens them.
>
> CCC 234

INQUIRY Q3

Q3

In Short:

- The Trinity comprises three persons in one God.
- The Trinity is revealed through Scripture.
- Through the Trinity, you have a relationship with each person.

The Holy Trinity

Do you know someone who's never seen without his or her "other half," no matter what? A pair who, when you think about one, the other person always comes to mind? Is it a couple? Best friends? Siblings? Whatever the relationship, these two share a lot of similar traits. They probably have the same interests and hobbies, use the same expressions, think the same way, they may even look alike! They're also probably together a lot, too. In fact, they may only be so similar because they care about each other and spend time together.

While this isn't the same as God in the Trinity, the three in one, these kinds of relationships help us better understand—in human terms—this mystery of faith and the love they share. Because we are created in the image of God, we are able to enter into communion with others (*CCC* 357). It is often through our human relationships—in marriage, family, church, or the wider human community—that we experience the love of God.

- *What relationships or communities have helped you to experience God's love?*

God Is Love

What was God doing before he created the world? The answer can be found in the doctrine of the **Holy Trinity**. The *Catechism* captures the heart of this mystery in one short phrase: "God is one but not solitary" (*CCC* 254). There is truly only one God, but even before the creation of the universe, this one God was three persons, eternally united in a communion of love. God was not, is not, and never will be lonely or bored, for he is eternally loving: the Father loving the Son, the Son loving the Father, and the Spirit proceeding from and sharing in that love.

Within its own divine being, the Trinity is a loving union. The Apostle John declares, "God is love" (1 John 4:8). "By sending his only Son and the Spirit of Love in the fullness of time, God has revealed his innermost secret: God himself is an eternal exchange of love, Father, Son and Holy Spirit, and he has destined us to share in that exchange" (*CCC* 221).

Revelation of the Trinity

This inner secret of who God is was not revealed all at once, but gradually, step by step. Like children moving from grade to grade toward high school, humanity was led slowly toward a fuller knowledge of God.

TEENS

© 2023 Liguori Publications. Photocopying prohibited

CCC 221, 232–267, 357, 683–69, 730–32; 1082; 1110

The Holy Trinity

- Read the introductory text with your class. Ask participants to share related examples.
- Share an experience or person who helped to show you God's love and invite participants to do the same. *Remind participants that, while these examples may help us to better understand the mystery of the Trinity, no human example or metaphor can fully reflect or accurately describe it.*

Revelation of the Trinity

- After reading this section, ask participants to discuss why God may have chosen to reveal his true nature in steps. Make sure to clarify that God was always a triune God and that this belief is supported by Scripture (also covered in Q6).
- Discuss which person of the Trinity is the easiest to pray/talk to, then discuss the most difficult one. Recommend participants try to get to know the member of the Trinity they find most distant.

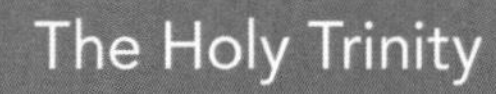

The Catechism quotes the fourth-century Church father St. Gregory of Nazianzus:

> *"The Old Testament proclaimed the Father clearly, but the Son more obscurely. The New Testament revealed the Son and gave us a glimpse of the divinity of the Spirit. Now the Spirit dwells among us and grants us a clearer vision of himself....By advancing and progressing 'from glory to glory,' the light of the Trinity will shine in ever more brilliant rays."*
>
> CCC 684

Step One

First the Father revealed himself to ancient Israel in the Old Testament. In a world that worshiped many gods and goddesses, he taught the ancient Israelites that he was the one and only God who created and rules the world. Even in the Old Testament, however, there were hints of the Trinity. The one God created the world "by the breath of his mouth" (Psalm 33:6). The Word (or Wisdom) of God and his life-giving Spirit (or Breath) were active in the Old Testament but not yet recognized as divine persons.

Step Two

Next in this progressive unfolding was the revelation of the Son. The Gospel of John begins with the eternal divine Word:

> *"In the beginning was the Word, and the Word was with God, and the Word was God."*
>
> John 1:1

The Old Testament spoke of God's activity in the world in terms of his living and active Word. This Word has been revealed as God's eternal Son:

> *"And the Word became flesh and made his dwelling among us, and we saw his glory, the glory as of the Father's only Son, full of grace and truth."*
>
> John 1:14

We celebrate the Incarnation, God's becoming flesh and coming to dwell with humanity in the person of Jesus, at Christmas. God is like a father to all creation, but Jesus is the Son in a unique way. The title "Son" of God means that God is not merely "Father" as Creator but in the very life of God there is an eternal Father-Son relationship: Jesus said, "No one knows the Son except the Father, and no one knows the Father except the Son and anyone to whom the Son wishes to reveal him" (Matthew 11:27). The Son and Father are so close they share the one divine nature.

Step Three

The final step is the revelation of the Holy Spirit. In the Son, we begin to glimpse the Spirit. At the baptism of Jesus, there is a manifestation of each person of the Trinity. The Son is baptized. The Father speaks. The Spirit descends as a dove. As Jesus approaches the cross, he begins to speak to his disciples of the promised Spirit he will send (John 14:16–17, 26). Yet the Spirit remains something of a mystery to the apostles until the day of Pentecost. On Pentecost, the Holy Spirit is "manifested, given, and communicated as a divine person...On that day, the Holy Trinity is fully revealed" (CCC 731–732).

In the history of salvation, the three persons of the Trinity are revealed in order: Father, Son, and Spirit. In our own lives, there is often a similar process, but we don't always come to know one divine person after another in that same order. Some people come to know Jesus first and later develop a relationship with the Father. It can be difficult to grasp that the Spirit is a divine person. Through prayer, we can come to know the Trinity as a personal presence who guides and helps us.

- *How would you describe your relationship to each person of the Trinity? Who did you come to know first: Father, Son, or Spirit?*
- *Which relationship needs the most growth?*

Q3

Speaking of God: Trinitarian Vocabulary

The ancient Church Fathers and early councils of the Church developed a basic vocabulary to express the mystery of God as one and three. While this mystery is really beyond words, it helps to have a place to start when we're trying to tell others—or just explaining it to ourselves.

Substance: Terms like "substance, essence or nature" describe what God is (*CCC* 253). They point to a single, infinite, all-powerful, all-holy divine reality, which is God. If asked, "What is God?" we answer in the singular: "God is one divine substance, nature, or essence."

Person: The word "person" speaks of who God is. If asked, "Who is God?" we answer in the plural: "God is three divine persons: Father, Son and Holy Spirit."

Relation: That which distinguishes one person from another. The Father's relation to the Son is described as an eternal generation or begetting. The Father shares his divinity with the Son. The Son is related to the Father as the eternal and only begotten Son, wholly receiving his divine nature from the Father, like "light from light." The Spirit eternally proceeds from the union of Father and Son as their love. "It is the Father who generates, the Son who is begotten, and the Holy Spirit who proceeds" (*CCC* 254).

Responding to the Love of the Trinity

The goal of the Trinitarian actions in creation and history is to bring human beings to share in their love. "By the grace of Baptism 'in the name of the Father and of the Son and of the Holy Spirit,' we are called to share in the life of the Blessed Trinity" (*CCC* 265). Saint Paul expresses this experience of grace:

> *"When the fullness of time had come, God sent his Son, born of a woman...to ransom [us], so that we might receive adoption. As proof that you are children, God sent the spirit of his Son into our hearts, crying out, 'Abba, Father!'"*
>
> Galatians 4:4–6

One special place where we encounter this activity and experience our relationship to the Trinity is the celebration of the Mass. In the Eucharist, we turn toward the Father in praise and thanksgiving. Our praise to the Father is offered in union with the Son and his perfect sacrifice offered on the cross. The priest asks the Holy Spirit to come upon our gifts of bread and wine and transform them into the Body and Blood of Christ. He also asks in prayer for the Holy Spirit to unite us to God and one another as the living body of Christ (*CCC* 1082, 1110).

We also grow closer to the Trinity through prayer. You can try ending every prayer with a brief conversation with each person of the Trinity like you're talking to a friend.

If you don't feel comfortable with spontaneous prayer yet, here are some other traditional prayers to the persons of the Trinity you can try on your own:

- The Our Father and Glory Be
- The Jesus Prayer
- Come, Holy Spirit

Speaking of God: Trinitarian Vocabulary

- In groups, have participants create their own definitions and examples for **substance**, **person**, and **relation** to share with the class. *If you have time, you can allow groups to create an art project, mock encyclopedia entry, skit, or other creative way that will make the definition stick.* Clarify any misinterpretations you find. You can use *CCC* 253–256 as reference material.

Responding to the Love of the Trinity

- Hand out the copies of Trinity prayers to participants. Ask participants if they can think of any others or, if you have time and resources, create a list of other Trinity prayers and where participants can find them.

Allow participants time to finish the activity, then review as a class. Ask for any questions about what's confusing or what's hard to accept on faith.

Answers:

(1) God.

(2) persons.

(3) relation.

(4) God, persons, love.

INQUIRY

JOURNEY OF FAITH

Test your Trinitarian vocabulary by filling in the blanks:

Father, Son, and Spirit are one_______________.

Father, Son, and Spirit are three _______________.

Father, Son, and Spirit are distinguished by their_______________.

God is one_______________ in three_______________

who live in eternal_______________ with each other.

Journey of Faith for Teens: Inquiry, Q3 (826337)

The process by which adults are initiated into the Catholic faith throughout the United States is now called the OCIA—the Order of Christian Initiation of Adults. "Order" is a clearer translation of the Latin term for the process formerly known as the RCIA—the Rite of Christian Initiation of Adults. People preparing for baptism and reception into the Church celebrate several rites as part of the order to which those rites belong—an order whose mission is to journey in the faith. The US Conference of Catholic Bishops adopted the name change in 2021, with American dioceses introducing the name thereafter. For more information, please contact your local diocese.

Imprimi Potest: Stephen T. Rehrauer, CSsR, Provincial, Denver Province, the Redemptorists.

Imprimatur: "In accordance with CIC 827, permission to publish has been granted on March 29, 2016, by the Most Reverend Edward M. Rice, Auxiliary Bishop, Archdiocese of St. Louis. Permission to publish is an indication that nothing contrary to Church teaching is contained in this work. It does not imply any endorsement of the opinions expressed in the publication; nor is any liability assumed by this permission."

Journey of Faith for Teens © 2000, 2016 Liguori Publications, Liguori, MO 63057. All rights reserved. No part of this publication may be reproduced, distributed, stored, transmitted, or posted in any form by any means without prior written permission. To order, visit Liguori.org or call 800-325-9521. Liguori Publications, a nonprofit corporation, is an apostolate of the Redemptorists. To learn more about the Redemptorists, visit Redemptorists.com.

© 2023 Liguori Publications. Photocopying prohibited

Contributing writer: John L. Gresham, PhD.
Editors of 2016 edition: Theresa Nienaber and Pat Fosarelli, MD, DMin.
Design: Lorena Mitre Jimenez. Images: Shutterstock.

Scripture texts in this work are taken from the *New American Bible*, revised edition ©2010, 1991, 1986, 1970 Confraternity of Christian Doctrine, Washington, D.C., and are used by permission of the copyright owner. All Rights Reserved. No part of the New American Bible may be reproduced in any form without permission in writing from the copyright owner. Excerpts from English translation of the *Catechism of the Catholic Church* for the United States of America © 1994 United States Catholic Conference, Inc. —*Libreria Editrice Vaticana*; English translation of the Catechism of the Catholic Church: Modifications from the Editio Typica © 1997 United States Catholic Conference, Inc. —*Libreria Editrice Vaticana*. Compliant with *The Roman Missal, Third Edition*.

Printed in the United States of America.
Third Edition.

Liguori PUBLICATIONS
A Redemptorist Ministry

Journey OF Faith

Journaling

Write a short prayer (or letter, poem, or picture) to each person of the Trinity.

Closing Prayer

End with the *O Sanctissima* (a prayer to the Trinity).

O most Holy Trinity, I adore you who dwell by your grace in my soul. Sanctify me more and more, make me love you more and more, abide with me evermore and be my true joy. Amen.

Looking Ahead

Jesus is not only one person in the Trinity he is also fully divine and fully human. Spend time this week thinking about that mystery. Have participants search online for Scripture references to Jesus' fully divine and fully human nature to share with the class (remind them to try to find verses that come from the *New American Bible*).

Q4: Who Is Jesus Christ?

Catechism: 514–682

Objectives

- Define Jesus as fully human and fully divine.
- Discover that Christ is the way to the Father and salvation.
- Develop participants' relationship with Jesus through personal sharing and reflection.

Leader Meditation

John 10:7–18

Jesus likens himself to a caring shepherd who would lay down his life for his sheep. Reflect on what these words tell us about the person Jesus.

Leader Preparation

- Read the lesson, this lesson plan, the Scripture passage, and the *Catechism* sections.
- Be familiar with the vocabulary terms for this section: *ichthys*, miracle, Messiah. Definitions are given in the lesson and in this guide's glossary.
- Be prepared to model and review the steps to looking up Bible verses. There are many in this lesson. Determine ahead of time whether you can cover them all as a group, will divide them up for groups, or will leave some for participants to reflect on outside of the session.
- Reach out to your pastor for guidance on possible questions or concerns surrounding Jesus' life, identity, words, and dual natures. Perhaps he can help to lead the session or recommend some quality apologetic material on these subjects.

Welcome

As participants arrive, welcome any new inquirers and sponsors. Check for supplies and immediate needs. Ask for any questions or comments about last week's lesson that may have come up during the week. Begin promptly.

Opening Scripture

John 10:7–18

Ask a volunteer to light the candle and read aloud. Ask participants what this passage tells us about Jesus. Focus on the importance of Jesus' words, "I am the good shepherd. I know my own and my own know me." Before beginning your discussion of the lesson handout, ask participants to think about ***who are Jesus' "own?"***

> As Lord, Christ is also head of the Church, which is his Body. Taken up to heaven and glorified after he had thus fully accomplished his mission, Christ dwells on earth in his Church.
>
> CCC 669

In Short:

- Jesus is fully human and fully divine.
- Christ is the way to the Father and salvation.
- Your relationship with Jesus grows through sharing and reflection.

Who Is Jesus Christ?

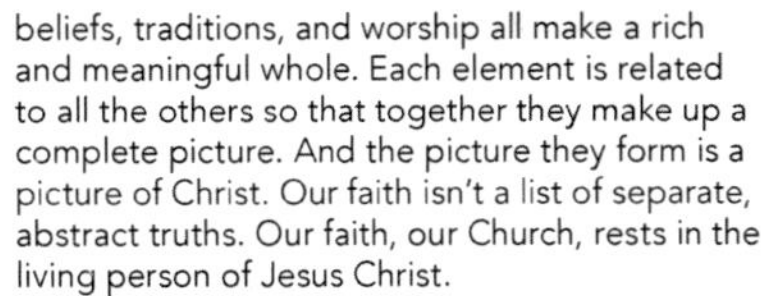

What do you see in the image at right? Early Christians used the fish symbol as a secret code indicating they were followers of Jesus. Sometimes the fish's eye was a tiny cross. You also see the Greek acronym **ichthys**. Each letter (*iota, chi, theta, upsilon, sigma*) begins the words in the title "Jesus Christ, Son of God, Savior." When early Christians saw the fish or ichthys, they knew immediately they had met another Christian and were safe from persecution. They belonged to each other and to the Lord.

Like the Jesus fish, the Catholic Church is made up of many elements that illustrate deeper truths. In the case of the Jesus fish, these elements are letters that stand for a greater message. In the case of the Church, these elements are doctrines and beliefs, prayers, and liturgies, and a vast and diverse community of believers. When looked at separately, doctrines, prayers, and individuals give us only a glimpse of the Church.

But when we stand back and look at the big picture, we can see how the Church's doctrines, beliefs, traditions, and worship all make a rich and meaningful whole. Each element is related to all the others so that together they make up a complete picture. And the picture they form is a picture of Christ. Our faith isn't a list of separate, abstract truths. Our faith, our Church, rests in the living person of Jesus Christ.

How Do We Come to Know the Person Jesus Christ?

Two thousand years ago, there were no devices to record the words and actions of Jesus or the internet to spread his message quickly. Reports could only be spread by word of mouth. Nonetheless, we might expect that the **miracles** recorded later in the Gospels would have exploded throughout the known world.

Although Jesus was mentioned by both Jewish and pagan historians, most of what we know about him comes from the Gospels. You and many others may wonder why this is. If Jesus really did perform all those miracles and everything else the Gospel writers claim, why did his life end in humiliation? And why didn't more people write about a man doing such extraordinary things?

The answer is that while Jesus was extraordinary, he wasn't extraordinary in the way the Jews of his time expected the **Messiah** to be. They were awaiting the Messiah, their savior, but a Messiah who came as a mighty warrior. They never imagined their savior would be born into near poverty, the son of a simple carpenter. It took years for the followers of Jesus to realize who he was, so it's not surprising Jesus went unrecognized by so many. It's no wonder few could accept him as the long-awaited savior.

TEENS

© 2023 Liguori Publications. Photocopying prohibited

CCC 514–682

Who Is Jesus Christ?

- Discuss the introductory image and text. Ask participants why the fish symbol was important to early Christians and why it is still used by Christians today.

How Do We Come to Know the Person Jesus Christ?

- As you read about the different portrayals of Jesus in the Gospels, talk about the difference between portraits and photographs.
- Ask participants what a portrait offers that a photograph doesn't (and vice versa). Remind participants that, like the other books of the Bible, the Gospels were divinely inspired. So while they might offer different perspectives on Jesus, they still reflect a greater truth in common.
- If you have time, create your own portrait of Jesus as a class, or just list elements that you'd include in one.
- Have participants answer the question why some Jews weren't ready to accept Jesus as the Messiah. Discuss how we respond when things in life don't match our expectations.

The True Identity of Jesus

Spend time going over the depictions of Jesus in the listed Gospel passages. If you can, split your class into groups and have each group take one or two to share.

- John 4:25–26
"I am he, the one who is speaking with you."

- Matthew 19:28–29
"Anyone who has given up something for the sake of Jesus' name will receive it a hundred times over and inherit eternal life."

- John 8:12
"I am the light of the world."

- Luke 15:1–7
"Jesus refers to himself as the shepherd who would go after a single lost sheep."

INQUIRY

JOURNEY OF FAITH

Even the Gospel stories were not recorded until years after the death of Jesus. Each Gospel came from a distinct oral tradition (see Q5, "The Bible"), some of them from more than one, and each Gospel was written for a different audience. For this reason, when we study the four Gospels, we find four unique portraits of the man Jesus. Unlike a photo that gives us an exact likeness, a portrait reflects the artist's unique understanding of the subject and is able to give us a glimpse into the subject's personality through the artist. When we study the four Gospel portraits, we get a very good idea of who Jesus was, the things he valued, and the truths he taught, but they aren't exact transcripts of everything Jesus said and did.

- *Why do you think some of the Jews weren't ready to accept Jesus as Messiah?*
- *Why were they disappointed in him?*

The True Identity of Jesus

Historical research has established the approximate date of Jesus' birth, the place, and so on. These are the details we commonly use to establish the identity of any ordinary person. But Jesus was no ordinary person. These details don't explain why the Christian faith is among the most popular in the world. The historical facts about Jesus don't explain why, thousands of years after his death, he continues to influence the lives of so many.

The Gospels themselves are largely unconcerned with historical facts. They aren't concerned with describing what Jesus looked like, what he wore, or what he possessed. The authors of the Gospels were only interested in telling us who Jesus was and is so that we might come to know him and model our own lives after his.

In John's Gospel (the last to be written and therefore the one that most reflects the developing faith of the early Church), Jesus reveals important details about who he is.

How does Jesus describe himself in the following passages?

John 4:25–26	Matthew 19:28–29
John 8:12	Luke 15:1–7

Each of these passages tells us something very important about who Jesus is. In John 14:6–7, Jesus gives us everything necessary for our own happiness—both here on earth and eternally in heaven. He tells us that he is "the way and the truth and the life"—and to know him is to know God.

Jesus Is the Way

When meeting someone for the first time we often ask, "Where are you from?"

The fact that Jesus came from Nazareth was puzzling to those who met him. "Can anything good come from Nazareth?" (John 1:46). To those who followed him, Jesus gave this answer: "I came from the Father and have come into the world. Now I am leaving the world and going back to the Father" (John 16:28).

Jesus is "the Way" not only because of his teachings (which were already familiar to the Jews and found in the Old Testament) but because he is the Son of God. Through Jesus, we come to know and understand God. Christ's life reveals the goodness of God. This is what, through all of history, makes Jesus unique.

- *Is there a particular Gospel story that helps you better understand God? Why?*

Jesus Is the Way

- If you have time, let participants answer the reflection question in their prayer journals. If you're running short on time, ask students to think about this question in prayer at home.

Jesus Is the Truth

What do we mean when we say that Jesus reveals God to us? Do we mean that, because Jesus comes from God, he can give us inside information we can't get anywhere else? Not quite. He says: "I am the Truth," not "I speak the truth" or "I reveal the truth," but "I *am* the Truth."

Jesus had a message and he went about Palestine proclaiming it. But he didn't just ask people to believe his message; he asked them to believe in him. And this was something completely new. Unlike the prophets and teachers of the past, Jesus had not come merely as a messenger to tell people about God. In Jesus, God is made present to us all. In every word and action, Jesus reveals God to us. He shows us, in ways we can understand, the true nature of God.

This is particularly true in the miracles Jesus worked. Throughout the Gospels, Jesus is shown healing the sick, curing lepers, feeding thousands, even raising the dead. But Jesus did not perform miracles just to add authority to his teaching or to convince unbelievers. Nor did he perform them simply to demonstrate he had special power.

Far from using miracles to impress large crowds, Jesus performed most of them in the presence of only a few people, and he usually asked his disciples not to tell anyone about what they had seen. Jesus himself tells us, "The works that the Father gave me to accomplish, these works that I perform testify on my behalf that the Father has sent me" (John 5:36).

Jesus' miracles are signs of his mission, signs that God loves us and is present and at work in the world. They are signs that Jesus is "the Truth."

Truth is often difficult to recognize and even more difficult to accept. Truth demands that we take a close look at ourselves. Truth often asks that we grow and change.

- *Can you think of a time new information caused you to change your beliefs? Was it difficult or easy to accept? Why?*

Jesus Is the Life

We can never forget that the greatest treasure we have—life itself—is fragile. In the face of death, we are powerless, none of our earthly possessions matter. It was this awareness that made the Jewish people hunger for a savior. They longed for the gift of everlasting life.

At the start of his public preaching, Jesus said: "I came so that they might have life and have it more abundantly" (John 10:10). As time went on, he began to explain to his followers that the life that truly matters is life everlasting.

At Pentecost, Jesus sent the Holy Spirit so we might have the courage to follow him and be light for a dark world. Jesus knows how hard it is to be like him today. Instead of retaliation, we must forgive. Instead of hate, we must love. Instead of harboring prejudice, we must accept. Instead of seeking the company of those with money, fame, or power, we must protect and care for the poor. Instead of accumulating things, we must strive for simplicity. This is how we show that Jesus is "the Life."

These things are not only the keys to everlasting life, they are also the keys to human happiness here and now. In doing our best to be very like Jesus, we not only find everlasting life, we find—and are part of—the reign of God here on earth today.

Jesus Is the Truth

- Ask participants how learning a truth that conflicts with what you believe can be scary or how we determine whether or not something is true. Emphasize that we know Jesus is the truth and that Jesus as truth is the center of our faith.

Jesus Is the Life

- Ask participants to explain in their own words how Jesus can be both fully human and fully divine. Discuss what this means and emphasize that Jesus isn't half-human or half-divine but fully both.
- Emphasize to participants that Jesus is the key to true happiness today, but we have to live by faith to attain that happiness.

As a class or with a partner, pick two to three of the following Scripture stories and determine: (1) what the miracle is and (2) what that miracle might mean for your life.

Suggested responses for part 1 are given below. Responses for part 2 will vary by participant.

- Luke 1:26–38; 2:1–7
Jesus is born of the Holy Spirit and the Virgin Mary at Nazareth.

- John 2:1–11
Turning water into wine during the Wedding at Cana.

- Matthew 8:1–4
The cleansing, or healing, of a man with leprosy.

- Luke 7:1–10
The healing of the centurion's slave.

- Mark 5:21–43
Healing of the hemorrhaging woman and raising the synagogue official's daughter from the dead.

- Luke 9:12–17
The multiplication of the loaves and the fish.

- Matthew 14:22–33
Jesus enables Peter to walk on water for as long as he has faith.

JOURNEY OF FAITH | INQUIRY

As a class or with a partner, pick two or three of the following Scripture stories and determine:

(1) what the miracle is and (2) what that miracle might mean for your life.

Luke 1:26–38; 2:1–7 | John 2:1–11 | Matthew 8:1–4 | Luke 7:1–10 | Mark 5:21–43 | Luke 9:12–17 | Matthew 14:22–33

Jesus left his followers with these beautiful words of wisdom and hope:

"If you remain in my word, you will truly be my disciples, and you will know the truth, and the truth will set you free."
John 8:31–32

What does it mean to you to be a disciple of Jesus? How does your relationship with Jesus impact your life?

Journey of Faith for Teens: Inquiry, Q4 (826337)
The process by which adults are initiated into the Catholic faith throughout the United States is now called the OCIA—the Order of Christian Initiation of Adults. "Order" is a clearer translation of the Latin term for the process formerly known as the RCIA—the Rite of Christian Initiation of Adults. People preparing for baptism and reception into the Church celebrate several rites as part of the order to which those rites belong—an order whose mission is to journey in the faith. The US Conference of Catholic Bishops adopted the name change in 2021, with American dioceses introducing the name thereafter. For more information, please contact your local diocese.

Imprimi Potest: Stephen T. Rehrauer, CSsR, Provincial, Denver Province, the Redemptorists.

Imprimatur: "In accordance with CIC 827, permission to publish has been granted on March 29, 2016, by the Most Reverend Edward M. Rice, Auxiliary Bishop, Archdiocese of St. Louis. Permission to publish is an indication that nothing contrary to Church teaching is contained in this work. It does not imply any endorsement of the opinions expressed in the publication; nor is any liability assumed by this permission."

Journey of Faith for Teens © 2000, 2016 Liguori Publications, Liguori, MO 63057. All rights reserved. No part of this publication may be reproduced, distributed, stored, transmitted, or posted in any form by any means without prior written permission. To order, visit Liguori.org or call 800-325-9521. Liguori Publications, a nonprofit corporation, is an apostolate of the Redemptorists. To learn more about the Redemptorists, visit Redemptorists.com.

© 2023 Liguori Publications. Photocopying prohibited

Contributing writer: John L. Gresham, PhD.
Editors of 2016 edition: Theresa Nienaber and Pat Fosarelli, MD, DMin.
Design: Lorena Mitre Jimenez. Images: Shutterstock.

Scripture texts in this work are taken from the *New American Bible*, revised edition ©2010, 1991, 1986, 1970 Confraternity of Christian Doctrine, Washington, D.C., and are used by permission of the copyright owner. All Rights Reserved. No part of the New American Bible may be reproduced in any form without permission in writing from the copyright owner. Excerpts from English translation of the *Catechism of the Catholic Church* for the United States of America © 1994 United States Catholic Conference, Inc. —*Libreria Editrice Vaticana*; English translation of the Catechism of the Catholic Church: Modifications from the Editio Typica © 1997 United States Catholic Conference, Inc. —*Libreria Editrice Vaticana*. Compliant with *The Roman Missal, Third Edition*.

Printed in the United States of America.
Third Edition.

Liguori PUBLICATIONS A Redemptorist Ministry

Journey of Faith

Journaling

What does it mean to you to be a disciple of Jesus? How does your relationship with Jesus impact your life?

Closing Prayer

Teach and pray aloud one of the memorial acclamations below. Explain that these statements summarize our faith and declare who Jesus is. They are so important, they are sung or recited (proclaimed) by the entire assembly at every Mass (our communal worship and central prayer).

We proclaim your Death, O Lord,
and profess your Resurrection
until you come again.

When we eat this Bread and
drink this Cup,
we proclaim your Death, O Lord,
until you come again.

Save us, Savior of the world,
for by your Cross and
Resurrection
you have set us free.

Looking Ahead

Over the next week, have participants read *John 1:1–18*, reflecting on what it means for Jesus to be God's Word incarnate. Catholics believe that Jesus is present throughout the entire Bible and that all of Scripture is fulfilled in the person of Christ. When we say the word of God is living, we refer to Christ (see *CCC* 102–103, 134).

Q5: The Bible

Catechism: 74–83; 101–133; 109–119

Objectives

- Identify and describe the historicity, structure, and nature of the Bible.
- Define Scripture as the sacred and inspired word of God.
- Discover that God speaks to and guides us through his word and the Church.
- Distinguish between proper and improper ways to use and interpret Scripture.
- Find any verse in the Catholic Bible.

Leader Meditation

2 Timothy 3:16–17

Reflect on these questions, then pray the prayer below. Do I take sufficient time each week to read and reflect on Scripture? When and how has God guided me through this sacred text, led me, and helped me make decisions about my life?

Dear God, you have given me the task of helping these young people understand your word. At times, I still struggle to understand it fully myself. Please send your Spirit to inspire and speak through me now, that I may become a bridge that connects your heart to the hearts and minds of my participants. Amen.

Leader Preparation

- Read the lesson, this lesson plan, the Scripture passage, and the *Catechism* sections.
- Be familiar with the vocabulary terms for this section: Scripture, Torah, epistles, psalm, divinely inspired, context, salvation history, Testament, inerrant. Definitions can be found in this guide's glossary.
- Make sure each participant has a Catholic Bible for the session and at home. Also gather materials and resources that assist them in studying and reflecting on Scripture and the Mass readings. If you can't provide physical Bibles for participants, give them a list of trusted Catholic translations and whether or not they can be found online.

Welcome

Greet participants as they arrive. Check for supplies and immediate needs. Solicit questions or comments about the previous session and/or share new information and findings. Begin promptly.

Opening Scripture

2 Timothy 3:16–17

Ask a participant to light the candle and read aloud. Afterward, allow a moment of silence and then ask for comments or reactions to the words. Before beginning your discussion of the lesson handout, ask participants, "How does the word of God equip us for good works?"

> Sacred Scripture is the speech of God as it is put down in writing under the breath of the Holy Spirit...[It] must be read and interpreted in the light of the same Spirit by whom it was written.
>
> *Dei Verbum*, 9, 12; see *CCC* 81, 111

INQUIRY Q5

In Short:

- The Bible has a unique history and nature.
- Scripture is the inspired word of God.
- Scripture must be interpreted carefully.

The Bible

When the pastor of a southwest Colorado parish asked his newly ordained associate to be present with him at each of the weekend Masses, the new priest welcomed the idea. It would be a great way for him to get a glimpse of the diverse groups of people he would be serving.

The youth choir led the music at the Saturday evening Mass for an assembly largely made up of young people, many of whom came with their friends. At the beginning of his homily, the pastor had the entire church laughing with a humorous story. Then he related the Gospel reading directly to the lives of young people.

At the 8 AM Mass on Sunday morning, the pastor led a senior and middle-aged assembly in the singing of traditional hymns. While the pastor's homily stressed the same truths, he was brief and took a no-frills approach.

The celebration at 10 AM was a different experience as well. The assembly of old and young prayed and sang in both Spanish and English.

There was much handholding and hugging among the gathered faithful. The homily also stressed the same message but focused on issues specific to the parish's Spanish-speaking community.

At the end of the weekend, the young priest marveled at how the pastor had brought the message of God's love to each one of the diverse groups in the way that best met them where they were in life.

The Bible was written with this same purpose in mind: sharing God's truth with every kind of Christian. The Bible:

- Delivers important truths about God.
- Tells us about the history of our faith and our **salvation history**.
- Reveals God's promise of everlasting life.

Like the parish pastor did in the story, the Bible's task is to deliver God's message of love to many different groups of people; in fact, *to all people for all ages!* You may be very familiar with the Bible, or you may only have a passing knowledge of some of the stories. Either way, today is an opportunity to discover the Bible in a new way.

What Is the Bible?

The **Bible** is a collection of books and writings by many different authors. Many of these stories were passed down from generation to generation by word of mouth long before anyone wrote the stories down. When the stories were written down, the authors came from different backgrounds, so the books originated with a variety of languages. These stories, also called **Scriptures**, were all written for different reasons but have the common purpose to try to share the

TEENS

© 2023 Liguori Publications. Photocopying prohibited

CCC 74–83; 101–133; 109–119

Q5

The Bible

- Read the Q5 introductory anecdote together. Ask participants what stood out to them about the story. Invite them to offer experiences where a priest, minister, or teacher has done this well or poorly.

What Is the Bible?

- Discuss how participants approached (or didn't) the Bible before coming to the OCIA. This will help you get a baseline for how familiar participants are with the Bible or how their former perspective may be at odds with Catholic teaching (such as taking the Bible as historical and scientific fact in all cases).

How Is the Bible Divinely Inspired?

- Participants may ask questions about the reliability of Scriptures *(questions may include: if Scripture is fiction or a fictionalized account, if Scripture is biased by the writers or the translators who were influenced by Church leaders, how accounts might have evolved over retellings and oral tradition…).* There is evidence both within Scriptures themselves and outside of it that roots them to historical events and eyewitness accounts. Encourage curious participants to continue exploring Catholic resources on the history of the Bible *(CCC Article 3: Sacred Scripture is a good place to start.)*
- While the Bible should not be discussed as fiction, you should also explain the difficulties of using the Bible as a science text.

  For example: Genesis teaches important truths about our faith and creation, but it wasn't written to give us a scientific explanation of creation. That was never its purpose. One way to think about it is that while Genesis doesn't tell us in scientific language how the world was created, it does explain why the world was created and who created it.

- Ask participants to discuss how the Bible is inerrant. Take this time to clarify any confusion and emphasize that the Bible teaches truth and is divinely inspired.

INQUIRY

JOURNEY OF FAITH

story of God's relationship with his people. The story of our faith and of our relationship with the one, true God is also called our salvation history.

How Is the Bible Divinely Inspired?

When we say the books of the Bible were written under the inspiration of the Holy Spirit, or **divinely inspired**, we mean that God in some way influenced the work of the authors. That doesn't mean God dictated the books word for word to biblical authors. It means that the authors allowed the Holy Spirit to work through them. Through these authors, God shares with us what we need to know for our salvation, our eternal life with God.

The Catholic Church believes that readers of the Bible must keep the meaning or purpose of a particular passage in mind rather than accepting every passage as literal fact. The Church, with the help of Scripture scholars, makes a distinction between truth and fact. While the Bible is **inerrant** (without mistakes) with regard to the truths it teaches because it has been divinely inspired, everything in the Bible is not fact.

For example, Genesis is not meant to be read as a scientific description of creation. It was a profession of faith in the goodness of God and his creation. These are the truths we learn from the first several chapters of Genesis:

- God created the world.
- Everything God created was good.
- Man and woman were created in the image and likeness of God.
- Man and woman are the caretakers, or stewards, of God's magnificent creation.
- God's love for man and woman is perfect.

How Is the Bible Organized?

The Bible is divided into the Old Testament and the New Testament. The word **testament** means "agreement" or "covenant." The Old Testament is a collection of sacred writings about the covenant between God and our Jewish ancestors in faith, the Israelites. These books were written over a period of about 900 years, and they record important events and experiences of the Israelite people as they come to know Yahweh, the one true God.

The New Testament is about God's covenant—through Jesus Christ—with God's people. The New Testament doesn't replace the Old Testament, it's the continuation and fulfillment. That's why it can be hard to fully grasp the meaning of the New Testament without knowledge of the Old Testament.

Read Exodus 19:3–8.

- *What did God promise our ancestors in faith in this covenant?*

The Old Testament

The books of the Old Testament can be grouped to help us understand the journey of God's Chosen People. Each book has a particular purpose and was written in a unique style. There are forty-six books in the Old Testament of the *New American Bible*, revised edition (also called the *NABRE*).

- The **Pentateuch** ("five books" in Greek), is the first five books of the Old Testament. It is sometimes called the **Torah**, meaning "Law." While Moses is said to be the author of the Torah, these books come from many generations of oral tradition and tell us about the journey of the Israelites to become the people of God through Abraham.
- The **Historical Books** contain poetry, proverbs, and songs, all of which study the meaning of life. They look at the same issues we struggle with today: human suffering, human destiny, good and evil, and right and wrong.
- The **Prophetic Books**, through divine inspiration, speak for God about important situations facing the Israelites. The prophets often speak of the need for repentance and the coming of the Messiah.

Read Hebrews 10:15–18.

- *What are some of the promises of the new covenant?*

How Is the Bible Organized

- Use the reflection question to give participants practice looking up and interpreting Scripture as a group (Exodus 19:3–8). If you have time, walk participants through how to look up this reading from finding the correct book, to identifying where chapter and verse numbers occur within the text.

The Old Testament

- As you read through this section, make sure participants have a Bible too look through. As you discuss the books, invite participants to turn to that section in their Bible to become more familiar with it.
- Find Hebrews 10:15–18 as a class and give participants time to respond to the reflection question on their own.

Suggested responses include: God will forgive sins, and God's laws will be written on our hearts and minds.

The New Testament

After the resurrection of Jesus, his followers spread the good news by preaching. There were several years of oral tradition before the early Christians preserved their words in writing. By the end of the first century after Christ, nearly every one of the twenty-seven books of the New Testament were written.

- The **four Gospels** are portraits of Jesus that come from different oral traditions and were written for different communities. Each gives us unique insight into the person Jesus.
- The **Acts of the Apostles** is an account of how the early Christian communities lived and grew.
- The **thirteen Pauline epistles**, or letters, and the **Book of Hebrews** are attributed to St. Paul or his followers.
- The **seven Catholic letters** are attributed to other apostles.
- The **Book of Revelation** was composed as a message of hope for Christians who were being persecuted. It is often misinterpreted as a prediction of the future, but its actual purpose was and is to comfort Christians with the promise of Christ's ultimate victory over suffering and evil.

How Do We Find Out the Meaning of Biblical Passages?

The first thing we do is look at context, when something was written, and the surrounding text. When verses from the Bible are interpreted without looking at these elements, we risk taking them out of context and misunderstanding them.

We must also understand the time and culture of the biblical author. Remember that the biblical world was very different from our own; it must be studied and understood if the full message of the Bible is to come through. The parable of the Prodigal Son (Luke 15:11–32) becomes even more meaningful if we understand its context. While we realize the father in this story is a loving and forgiving man, the extent of his love becomes even greater when we learn that upstanding men of Jesus' time never ran. Running was considered undignified and humiliating. This makes the father running to greet his son an even more powerful statement of unconditional love.

Knowing the literary form of a particular book of the Bible is also important. The Bible contains many literary forms: historical documentaries, epics, stories and parables, poems, hymns and songs, laws, letters, wisdom writing, prophecies, teachings, and prayers. Each form of writing has its own purpose and truth. If you can identify the form, it will help you understand the message God is communicating through the human author.

- *Can you recall a time when you were misunderstood because others failed to get the whole story or took something you said or did out of context?*

How Does the Church Help Us Understand the Bible?

Even with good knowledge of Scripture, we can sometimes be confused by passages that don't seem to fit in with Christ's message of love and forgiveness. When we take literary form and proper context into account, these passages make sense.

However, we must also realize that the faith of the Church grew and developed; it changed. The Old Testament and the New Testament were written over a period of about 1,000 years. Many of the Hebrews' teachings grew and developed as their knowledge of God became clearer. If we study the New Testament carefully, we can trace growth in the faith of the disciples as well.

As you become familiar with the Bible, you might find passages that contradict the faith we follow today. Church teachings are important because they help guide our knowledge of God as it is revealed through sacred Scripture.

The same Spirit that guided those original authors of Scripture enlightens us today as we seek the truth in God's word.

The New Testament

- As you read through this section, make sure participants have a Bible too look through. As you discuss the books, invite participants to turn to that section in their Bible to become more familiar with it.

How Do We Find Out the Meaning of Biblical Passages?

- Ask participants what it means to take something out of context and how that causes confusion and misunderstanding. Discuss why it's important for us to keep Scripture in the context it was written.

Participants will practice looking things up in their Bibles by finding and interpreting the following passages:

Genesis 2:2

Mark 10:13

Psalm 8:2

Luke 19:1–10

1 Corinthians 13:4–8

INQUIRY

JOURNEY OF FAITH

To find a book in the Bible, look at the table of contents in the front for the page number where the book begins. Then look for the chapter you want to read. Once you're in the right chapter, look for the verse number. Practice by looking for the verses below.

What do they tell you about faith or God?

Genesis 2:2

Mark 10:13

Psalm 8:2

Luke 19:1–10

1 Corinthians 13:4–8

Reflect on one of your favorite Bible stories or passages. If you know how to locate it in your Bible, read it over again.

How do you interpret the passage?

Can the truth found in this passage be applied to your life today? How?

Journey of Faith for Teens: Inquiry, Q5 (826337)

The process by which adults are initiated into the Catholic faith throughout the United States is now called the OCIA—the Order of Christian Initiation of Adults. "Order" is a clearer translation of the Latin term for the process formerly known as the RCIA—the Rite of Christian Initiation of Adults. People preparing for baptism and reception into the Church celebrate several rites as part of the order to which those rites belong—an order whose mission is to journey in the faith. The US Conference of Catholic Bishops adopted the name change in 2021, with American dioceses introducing the name thereafter. For more information, please contact your local diocese.

Imprimi Potest: Stephen T. Rehrauer, CSsR, Provincial, Denver Province, the Redemptorists.

Imprimatur: "In accordance with CIC 827, permission to publish has been granted on March 29, 2016, by the Most Reverend Edward M. Rice, Auxiliary Bishop, Archdiocese of St. Louis. Permission to publish is an indication that nothing contrary to Church teaching is contained in this work. It does not imply any endorsement of the opinions expressed in the publication; nor is any liability assumed by this permission."

Journey of Faith for Teens © 2000, 2016 Liguori Publications, Liguori, MO 63057. All rights reserved. No part of this publication may be reproduced, distributed, stored, transmitted, or posted in any form by any means without prior written permission. To order, visit Liguori.org or call 800-325-9521. Liguori Publications, a nonprofit corporation, is an apostolate of the Redemptorists. To learn more about the Redemptorists, visit Redemptorists.com.

© 2023 Liguori Publications. Photocopying prohibited

Editors of 2016 edition: Theresa Nienaber and Pat Fosarelli, MD, DMin.
Design: Lorena Mitre Jimenez. Images: Shutterstock.

Scripture texts in this work are taken from the *New American Bible*, revised edition ©2010, 1991, 1986, 1970 Confraternity of Christian Doctrine, Washington, D.C., and are used by permission of the copyright owner. All Rights Reserved. No part of the New American Bible may be reproduced in any form without permission in writing from the copyright owner. Excerpts from English translation of the *Catechism of the Catholic Church* for the United States of America © 1994 United States Catholic Conference, Inc. —*Libreria Editrice Vaticana*; English translation of the Catechism of the Catholic Church: Modifications from the Editio Typica © 1997 United States Catholic Conference, Inc. —*Libreria Editrice Vaticana*. Compliant with *The Roman Missal, Third Edition*.

Printed in the United States of America.
Third Edition.

Journaling

Reflect on one of your favorite Bible stories or passages. If you know how to locate it in your Bible, read it over again. How do you interpret the passage? Can the truth found in this passage be applied to your life today? How?

Closing Prayer

Read Hebrews 4:12 aloud, then tell participants Scripture is not only for knowledge and reference but also for prayer. Conclude with this prayer:

God, may your words remain with me, in my mind, on my lips, and in my heart. May their message of love not depart, in sorrow or joy. For every joy has been written, and every sorrow has been consoled by your holy word.

Looking Ahead

Take time before the next session to ask participants to reflect on other ways the Holy Spirit speaks to us and teaches us about the nature of God and salvation.

Q6: Divine Revelation

Catechism: 27–100

Objectives

- Define revelation as the manifestation of God and his plan of salvation.
- List multiple ways God has revealed himself throughout history (including creation, Scripture, apostolic tradition, the Magisterium, and personal encounters).

Leader Meditation

John 16:13–15

Pray that you will grow in your openness to all God has revealed and his plan for your life.

Leader Preparation

- Read the lesson, this lesson plan, the Scripture passage, and the *Catechism* sections. Be prepared to answer questions about Church authority as it relates to sacred tradition.
- Be familiar with the vocabulary terms for this section: divine revelation, Magisterium, sacred tradition. Definitions are provided in this guide's glossary.

Welcome

Greet participants as they arrive. Check for supplies and immediate needs. Solicit questions or comments about the previous session and/or share new information and findings. Begin promptly.

Opening Scripture

John 16:13–15

Ask one of the participants to light the candle and read aloud. Afterward, allow a moment of silence and then welcome comments or reactions to the words. Before beginning your discussion of the lesson handout, ask participants, ***"What are some ways the Holy Spirit leads us to the truth about God? About our own lives?"***

The People of God as a whole never ceases to welcome, to penetrate more deeply, and to live more fully from the gift of divine Revelation.

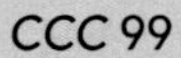

CCC 99

INQUIRY Q6

In Short:

- Revelation teaches us about God and salvation.
- Human nature teaches us about God.
- Divine revelation comes from many sources.

Divine Revelation

Getting to Know God

There are two true and certain ways we can come to know God as a person: creation (which includes the cosmos and our human experience) and divine revelation.

When we think about creation, three questions come to mind:

1. What/Who created the universe and when?
2. What controls creation as it continues to develop?
3. What's the meaning of life, the universe, and everything, anyway? As we try to find answers to these questions, we begin to learn more about God. As God reveals more to us, he relies on our ability to think about what we can observe to discern his truth.

Knowing God Through Human Nature

Humans are, by nature, religious beings (see *CCC* 27–28). Put another way, God created all humans—not just Catholics or Christians—to know God. It's in our spiritual DNA. Saint Paul says God "wills everyone to be saved and to come to knowledge of the truth" (1 Timothy 2:4). Saint Augustine famously wrote, "Our heart is restless until it rests in [God]" (*Confessions* 1,1,1:PL 32, 659–661).

God created us out of love, put love inside us, and wants us to live in love with him for eternity. To satisfy our thirst for love and God, we seek out truth and joy and long to fill our lives with them. When we're searching for truth but don't know God, it's like feeling around in the dark for a light. When we know God, he illuminates the truth for us.

- *Give an example of when you "knew" something was real or fake. It could be a promise, a story someone told you, a friendship, or other example. How did you know?*
- *Describe a time when you felt completely at peace. What truths might be hidden there?*

TEENS

© 2023 Liguori Publications. Photocopying prohibited

CCC 27–100

Knowing God Through Human Nature

- Emphasize how what we know about science and creation can also help us encounter God (science doesn't take away the mystery and wonder of God; it helps us see his mystery and wonder in new ways).
- Discuss the first reflection question (give an example of when you "knew" something was real) as a group. As participants share examples, ask if or how faith played a role in that knowledge or if any of those examples are similar to how participants came to "know" joining the Catholic Church was the right decision.
- Read Psalm 139 as a class. Give participants time to answer the reflection question in their journals.

Divine Revelation

- After reading the short introduction, have participants talk about times they have encountered God in creation (on a walk, on vacation, in a profound moment with a relative or friend). Be prepared to share a moment of significance to you or give an example from each of the four ways below (see *CCC* 31–38, 54–67):

The world: *nature, the universe, the laws of science*

The human person: *personal desires, experiences, relationships*

Scripture: *protection of the Israelites, fulfillment of prophecies in the Old Testament, Jesus' life and resurrection in the New Testament*

Sacred tradition: *papal and magisterial documents*

Knowing God Through Our Conscience

- If you have time, ask participants to share stories about when they've had to rely on their conscience to make a decision.

Knowing God Through Divine Revelation

- After reading the section, ask participants to explain public vs. private revelation in their own words. Clarify any confusion.

Sacred Scripture

- Discuss how Scripture can continue to teach us things today even though it was written long ago.

If participants have a difficult time understanding this concept, think about books, movies, or TV shows that, while created a long time ago, still speak to people today because of a focus on the human experience, such as relationships, going through a major life change, moving to an unfamiliar place, losing a friend, and other examples.

- If you have time, read Mark 2:1–12 and Luke 6:27–36 as a class and answer the reflection questions. Emphasize that these things: Christ's forgiveness, Jesus' teaching on love, hate, and our attitudes are examples of how Scripture can still apply to us today. *If you don't have time to do this in class, encourage participants to reflect on their own time.*

The spiritual life is foundational to a person's happiness. That life of the soul begins when we first realize that God is deeply connected to our personal, daily lives. There are a lot of things about ourselves we didn't choose: our gender, race, genetics, gifts, and talents. But God knew us before we were born.

> *"You formed my inmost being; you knit me in my mother's womb....My very self you know. My bones [were] not hidden from you, When I was being made in secret...."*
>
> Psalm 139:13–15

- *What does Psalm 139 teach me about my relationship with God?*

Knowing God Through Our Conscience

> *"With his openness to truth and beauty, his sense of moral goodness, his freedom and the voice of his conscience, with his longings for the infinite and for happiness, man...discerns signs of his spiritual soul."*
>
> CCC 33

We also come to know God and his love through our "inner voice of conscience." As the Lord says to Jeremiah, "I will place my law within [my people], and write it upon their hearts" (31:33). Morality, the true difference between right and wrong, is universal across history and cultures. That means civil laws and rules of behavior may vary, but a judgment between good and bad remains. Only God can give this gift.

Knowing God Through Divine Revelation

No matter how hard we try to know God and understand the mysteries of faith and the universe, when we try to get it on our own, our human knowledge is filled with missing pieces (see *CCC* 37).

- We may know God exists, that he's kind and merciful, and that he desires our salvation, but what does that really mean for me?
- Being human is complicated. Issues of morality, circumstances, and living well make doing the right thing a challenge. So how do I do what's right?
- Even when we try as hard as we can, sometimes we get it wrong. Does that mean there's something wrong with me?

Divine revelation is a public and historical act, distinct from private revelation. In his goodness, God gives us revelation to help us know those truths that reason can reach but not fully understand or hold onto. Everyone, including ordinary people and those under the negative impact of sin, can know God with ease and certainty, without the threat of error (*CCC* 38).

Sacred Scripture

> *"God has revealed himself to man by gradually communicating his own mystery in deeds and in words."*
>
> *CCC* 69

In Scripture, the word *revelation* means "the unveiling or uncovering of two basic realities":

1. Who God is.
2. Who the human person is.

When we talk about revelation, we are learning about God and his plan of salvation, which unfolds gradually over long periods of time. It comes to us through the events of history and is communicated in the words of men and women. Many of these events and figures are recorded within the books of the Bible. The Scriptures are inspired—literally "in-breathed"—by the Holy Spirit. God empowered each biblical author to speak and write in a way that would convey the truth to every generation.

Have you ever heard that the Bible doesn't apply to our century or culture? That it's impossible to live by? On a literal level, that's true. A lot of things people did in the Bible aren't done now, or they are done so differently it's hard to recognize. But this view takes the Bible only as a cultural artifact from long ago, not as the word of God to us right here and right now.

Scripture is more than just religious literature. It's the telling of God's inner life, an authentic witness to God's heart, mind, and will for us. When you read Scripture, you are hearing the voice of God. While we may not live in the same kinds of societies the Bible writers did, the truth of God's inner life and the truth of these Scriptures has stayed the same.

Sometimes we don't know or aren't sure when we've encountered the Lord. Ask God to help you discover his presence in your heart as you read the words of the Bible. This prayer may help:

Lord Jesus, you are the face of God. As I journey through your word and reflect on your covenants, help me to see your hand leading me to this moment just as you lead the people of Israel and the apostles after you. Guide me to the truth, and show me your plan for my salvation. Send me your Spirit, who inspired all of Scripture. Amen.

Knowing God Through the Magisterium and Sacred Tradition

Magisterium is a Latin word meaning "an authoritative voice." It refers to the Church's official and authentic teaching office, held by the pope and the bishops in union with him. Magisterial teaching is found in ecumenical councils (such as Vatican II, also known as the Second Vatican Council) and special papal pronouncements (such as encyclicals). The Magisterium hands down the truths about Jesus in a divine and prophetic way. When questions of faith and morality emerge or need clarification, the Spirit guides the Church to discern Christ's will and unfold its meaning in new and deeper ways. This is how revelation is handed on intact.

Sacred tradition starts with the New Testament. John 21:25 states that the Bible does not contain all that Jesus said and did. So where's the rest? It's in sacred tradition, which is the lived witness of the whole Church, formed under the leadership and teachings of the apostles and their successors, the bishops. To make sure that Jesus' words and deeds were handed on intact, the Holy Spirit assisted the apostles in choosing successors who would continue teaching them until Christ returns. This line of authentic, Spirit-filled transmission began with Jesus, proceeded through the apostles, formed the New Testament, and continues to our bishops today. Sacred tradition also includes all of our liturgies and creeds as well as the lives and teachings of the saints and doctors of the Church.

Mark 2:1–12: Jesus heals the paralytic as a proof that he has the authority and power to forgive sins.

- *Have you witnessed or experienced Christ's forgiveness? What effect did it have on you?*

Luke 6:27–36: How do Jesus' words about love, hate, and attitudes still apply to our lives today?

- *Think about a time when you acted out of anger or hate instead of with love. If your sorrow (contrition) or conscience leads you to ask for forgiveness, then do it! The Church offers reconciliation to those who approach Jesus in faith.*

Knowing God Through the Magisterium and Sacred Tradition

Some participants might struggle with understanding how the magisterium *is a necessary part of the Church and our faith. You may find it helpful to read through the* Dogmatic Constitution on Divine Revelation *(*Dei Verbum*) to help you answer participant questions. If there's something you don't feel you can answer accurately or adequately during class, meet with the participant after class or refer the person to someone or a resource that can answer the question.*

What do the following Scripture verses say about truth? *Student responses may vary, but some suggested responses appear below.*

- Psalm 85:11–12
The divine comes to earth in the form of love, truth, and justice.

- John 8:32
The truth frees us.

- John 18:38
Jesus is truth.

- 1 John 2:4
If we say we know Jesus but don't act like it, we are not acting with truth.

Student responses to questions one through four will vary.

INQUIRY

JOURNEY OF FAITH

What do the following Scripture verses say about truth?

Psalm 85:11–12:
"Love and truth will meet...
Truth will spring from the earth."

John 8:32:
"The truth will set you free."

John 18:38:
"What is truth?"

1 John 2:4:
"Whoever...does not keep God's commandments is a liar...the truth is not in him."

Are there any truths of the Church that you struggle to accept or understand? Why?

If you feel comfortable, share this question with a faith mentor, someone you trust who can help faithfully guide you in this question.

Ask God to speak to your heart as you answer these questions simply and honestly:

1. If I am made in the image and likeness of God (Genesis 1:26–27), how does that make me:
    a. Good?
    b. Unique?
    c. Powerful?
2. What are my best qualities and unique gifts?
3. How do I bring goodness to my...
    a. Family
    b. Friends
    c. School
    d. Community/Parish
4. What goodness do these people and communities give to me and what do they teach me about God? Give at least three examples.

Journey of Faith for Teens: Inquiry, Q6 (826337)
The process by which adults are initiated into the Catholic faith throughout the United States is now called the OCIA—the Order of Christian Initiation of Adults. "Order" is a clearer translation of the Latin term for the process formerly known as the RCIA—the Rite of Christian Initiation of Adults. People preparing for baptism and reception into the Church celebrate several rites as part of the order to which those rites belong—an order whose mission is to journey in the faith. The US Conference of Catholic Bishops adopted the name change in 2021, with American dioceses introducing the name thereafter. For more information, please contact your local diocese.

Imprimi Potest: Stephen T. Rehrauer, CSsR, Provincial, Denver Province, the Redemptorists.

Imprimatur: "In accordance with CIC 827, permission to publish has been granted on March 29, 2016, by the Most Reverend Edward M. Rice, Auxiliary Bishop, Archdiocese of St. Louis. Permission to publish is an indication that nothing contrary to Church teaching is contained in this work. It does not imply any endorsement of the opinions expressed in the publication; nor is any liability assumed by this permission."

Journey of Faith for Teens © 2000, 2016 Liguori Publications, Liguori, MO 63057. All rights reserved. No part of this publication may be reproduced, distributed, stored, transmitted, or posted in any form by any means without prior written permission. To order, visit Liguori.org or call 800-325-9521. Liguori Publications, a nonprofit corporation, is an apostolate of the Redemptorists. To learn more about the Redemptorists, visit Redemptorists.com.

© 2023 Liguori Publications. Photocopying prohibited

Editors of 2016 edition: Theresa Nienaber and Pat Fosarelli, MD, DMin.
Design: Lorena Mitre Jimenez. Images: Shutterstock.

Scripture texts in this work are taken from the *New American Bible*, revised edition ©2010, 1991, 1986, 1970 Confraternity of Christian Doctrine, Washington, D.C., and are used by permission of the copyright owner. All Rights Reserved. No part of the New American Bible may be reproduced in any form without permission in writing from the copyright owner. Excerpts from English translation of the *Catechism of the Catholic Church* for the United States of America © 1994 United States Catholic Conference, Inc. —*Libreria Editrice Vaticana*; English translation of the Catechism of the Catholic Church: Modifications from the Editio Typica © 1997 United States Catholic Conference, Inc. —*Libreria Editrice Vaticana*. Compliant with *The Roman Missal, Third Edition*.

Printed in the United States of America.
Third Edition.

Journaling

Are there any truths of the Church that you struggle to accept or understand? Why? If you feel comfortable, share this question with a faith mentor, someone you trust who can help faithfully guide you in this question.

Closing Prayer

Read this prayer of St. Augustine (*CCC* 30) aloud:

You are great, O Lord, and greatly to be praised: great is your power and your wisdom is without measure. And man, so small a part of your creation, wants to praise you: this man, though clothed with mortality and bearing the evidence of sin and the proof that you withstand the proud. Despite everything, man, though but a small part of your creation, wants to praise you. You yourself encourage him to delight in your praise, for you have made us for yourself, and our heart is restless until it rests in you (see Confessions, Book 1, Chapter 1).

Looking Ahead

Before next class, have participants spend time in silence with the word of God. Keep your mind and heart open to what God might be trying to tell you.

Q7: Your Prayer Life

Catechism: 2558–65; 2725–45

Objectives

- Describe prayer as talking with God, formally or informally, individually or with a group.
- Identify basic forms and styles of Christian prayer.
- Practice new forms and styles of prayer.
- Evaluate what personal prayer style works best for them.

Leader Meditation

John 16:23–27; Matthew 18:19–20

Jesus tells us something very important about the power of prayer in each of these passages. Which modes of prayer are most comfortable for you? How much time do you spend in prayer preparing for these lessons?

Leader Preparation

- Read the lesson, this lesson plan, the Scripture passages, and the *Catechism* sections.
- Bring art supplies for participants to create their own prayer. If you're not doing this, try to find a space that will allow participants to spread out and reflect on the different prayer styles.

Welcome

Greet participants as they arrive. Check for supplies and immediate needs. Solicit questions or comments about the previous session and/or share new information and findings. Begin promptly.

Opening Scripture

John 16:23–27; Matthew 18:19–20

Ask for a volunteer to come to light the candle and read aloud. Afterward, allow a moment of silence, then welcome comments or reactions. Before beginning your discussion of the lesson handout, ask participants, ***"What important things does Jesus tell us about prayer in these readings? Why is it important for us to worship as a community of believers?"***

"Pray constantly" (1 Thessalonians 5:17). It is always possible to pray. It is even a vital necessity. Prayer and Christian life are inseparable.

CCC 2757

INQUIRY Q7

In Short:

- Prayer is talking with God.
- Prayer can be personal or done as part of a group.
- Prayer can be done in a variety of ways.

Your Prayer Life

Let's be honest. We don't always like to pray. There may be times we love to pray or feel invigorated by it, but we get distracted at Mass or in the middle of a rosary. We start to think about all the things we need to do—or all those things we'd rather be doing.

Does that mean we don't love God? No, but it does mean our love for God is immature. We have to discover the right way to pray for ourselves. Once we know that, it's easier to let God in to nourish our souls directly.

- *How do you feel about your prayer life?*
- *What about it would you change?*

School of Prayer

Prayer has a pretty broad definition. It's really anything we do that brings us into conversation with God. It can be a conversation, a common prayer like the Our Father, or any experience that makes you feel closer to God. We can pray to God when we want to praise him, we can petition God when we need something, we can give thanks to God for something good, and we can pray to God through the saints who intercede for us.

The following lessons aren't rules for prayer, they're more like guidelines to get you started. Explore and figure out what works best for you.

Lesson 1: It's OK to be Human
We may not feel thrilled every time we pray because feelings are as changeable as the weather. Prayer is precious not only because God touches our heart when we pray, but also because the quality of our prayer experience will not always be the same. How can we make our prayer life come alive?

Lesson 2: Give More, Not Less
When something bores us, we tend to put less and less time and energy into it. As we start to withdraw ourselves, it becomes even less interesting. We've probably all experienced this at school with a subject we don't particularly like.

One way to help prayer become more interesting is to throw ourselves into it anew, devoting more energy to it than before. We may speak to God more intimately and tell God straight out what we are thinking and feeling. We might try including prayer in all our activities—mowing the lawn, walking to school, preparing for tests....This will draw God and us together.

Lesson 3: Notice When You Feel Like Praying
It's true that discipline and duty have their place. But when we're trying to make our prayer come alive, it is wise to notice when we feel like praying.

TEENS

© 2023 Liguori Publications. Photocopying prohibited

CCC 2558–65; 2725–45

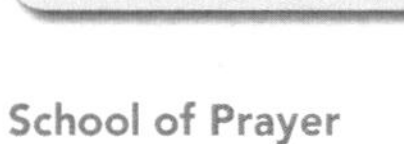

Your Prayer Life

- Before starting the lesson, ask participants what words or images come to mind when they think about prayer. If you can, collect these in a common place.
- After reading the lesson, discuss the reflection question as a group. Be prepared to share a story about growing in your own prayer life.
- Acknowledge that every participant has prayed before—even if he or she doesn't know it. In the OCIA process, participants will gain greater awareness of their communications with God and practice new and different kinds of prayer, like their use of a prayer or reflection journal during these classes.
- Emphasize that we do not always have to feel enthusiastic about praying for our prayer to be pleasing to God. Remind participants that God wants us to share anything and everything with him, and those things aren't always happy or joyful. It's OK to pray to God when we're sad, hurting, confused, or feeling alone as well as when we're happy, excited, and giving thanks.
- Clarify that in personal prayer, the only "wrong" way to pray is to pray with selfish intentions or to feign (fake) opening ourselves to God.

School of Prayer

- Read through each "lesson" together. After each, ask participants to suggest ways that guideline might strengthen someone's prayer life.

We should pray during those times and not push ourselves into it at other times. If we ask God to teach us to enjoy prayer, the Holy Spirit will plant the desire for prayer in our hearts. If we pay attention to the smallest desire and honor it by praying—maybe for only a few seconds—we will be drawn more and more to God.

God is faithful. God will not drive us or force us into prayer. God gently calls us. Our relationship with God is mutual, and that means we have to be faithful, too. While God won't force us to pray, we do need to answer in prayer when we feel God call.

Lesson 4: Pray Spontaneously
This means speaking to God or thinking about God without preparation, just as we speak to and think about one another. Sometimes, without meaning to, we separate ourselves from God because we attempt to put words together in just the right way or we try to think too profoundly about God. Praying spontaneously means sharing the little moments of our life with God. It means sharing our hearts with God when we are feeling sad about a troubled relationship or feeling the hurt of rejection. It means telling God about our anxiety moments before a big test or about our confusion when we are faced with difficult decisions.

Praying spontaneously means that we might say things to God that are more honest than nice or pleasant. Remember, God knows our hearts long before we can even find words to describe what we think and feel.

> *"Have no anxiety at all, but in everything, by prayer and petition, with thanksgiving, make your requests known to God."*
>
> Philippians 4:6

Lesson 5: Practice Regular Spiritual Reading
Our study of the Bible helps us know the Lord. Sometimes praying is like trying to communicate with a stranger. Knowledge of sacred Scripture turns that stranger into an acquaintance, then a friend, and finally a loved Father.

Reading Scripture slowly and seeking to understand it in small bits will empower our prayer. Often the very words of the Bible suddenly take on life, and we experience oneness with our Creator. The writings of the saints can also strengthen our prayer. Sometimes their lives are more like our own than we imagined. Many of them struggled with prayer, and their writings describe their personal faith journeys.

Spiritual reading gives us understanding and an awareness of the presence of God in the everyday places and people of our world.

Lesson 6: When Life Hurts, Say So
Practice talking to God any time, any place, and without a reason—just as you do with a best friend. When something bad (or good) happens in your life, who's the first person you call? Do you hesitate to complain or vent to your best friend? When your best friend does something that upsets you, do you let her or him know? Try thinking of God in the same way. When life doesn't go your way, when you're hurt and upset, tell God.

God doesn't mind if we pray to him when we're angry. In fact, he wants to know what's going on in our lives. God wants us to come to him in prayer no matter what we're feeling. God wants to listen to us just like our best friend does. As you start to think about God as someone to pray to, prayer will begin to seep into every part of your life. You don't have to reserve prayer for times when you're thankful or times when you need something; you can pray to God any time, no matter what you're feeling.

Lesson 7: Be Aware of God's Responses
While we may find ourselves able to speak comfortably to our Lord with a little effort and practice, it is quite another thing to develop the ability to listen to the Lord's responses. At one time or another, most of us have probably felt that God doesn't talk to us. It takes a long time to see that God always responds to us—we just usually miss the reply. To recognize God's answers to our prayers, we have to stretch inside.

The first stretch is giving up our expectations of what we think God will or should say. God doesn't communicate with us in ways we expect.

Listening to God doesn't mean that we'll get an immediate and obvious answer in words, visions, or directions. Listening sometimes means just opening our minds and hearts. It means *noticing* God's presence in our world and *recognizing* the Holy Spirit's activity.

Lesson 8: Don't Expect Quick Results
We need to remain very alert to gradual inner changes. Often the Holy Spirit works within our hearts, but changes don't happen overnight. When we come to God in prayer, we have to be patient. It can take a long time for our prayer to even feel like something spiritual, and it can take even longer to recognize God responding to those prayers.

We may find ourselves laughing at something that once really bothered us. Or we may feel an unexplainable gentleness or understanding toward someone we never liked. Compassion or peace may spring unexpectedly from our restless hearts. Old fears may melt away. These are the slow, subtle changes God works in our hearts as we pray.

New Forms of Prayer

Prayer doesn't have to be done the same way every time, and we don't have to pray the same way as someone else. Try some of the types of prayer below and find the one that works best for you.

Pray with your body. Our bodies often reflect what we feel inside. Think about what our body does when we run to greet a loved one we haven't seen for a long time. Think about how a mother cradles her child. What do the skipping feet of a child tell you about what she feels?

Try looking inside yourself. Imagine the feeling you want to express to God. Then allow your body to move as it will and offer this movement to God. You may even end up dancing before the Lord as King David did (2 Samuel 6:21). Dancing our prayer opens us even more to the Spirit within us.

Sing your prayer. Saint Augustine encourages us: "The one who sings prays twice." You may sing to the Lord familiar songs you know and love. Or you may spontaneously use your own words and melody. God doesn't care about beautiful voices. God cares about the heart. If singing to God enlivens your heart, then do it!

Write or draw your prayer. Many people pray through their journals. This can be a very effective expression of your thoughts and feelings to God. Your journal can be a completely private collection of letters to God, or it can be something you share with trusted friends or faith-sharing groups.

If you love to express yourself through art, try illustrating your journal prayers. Or use artwork alone to pray. Sometimes it is best to show God how we feel through our drawings, paintings, or sculptures.

Pray the news. Pray for and about the people and situations in the news, giving thanks for the good and asking for help for those who are suffering. Besides countering the negative feelings brought on by stories in the news media, this prayer relates the world to God and binds our own hearts to the compassionate Sacred Heart of Jesus.

Offer yourself as prayer. You can offer yourself to God without words by serving others or bearing burdens graciously. Practice offering yourself, not only in special times of prayer, but a thousand times a day in the midst of anything and everything. Soon you are living in God's presence most of the time and offering your very self to God in almost everything you do. What a great way to keep yourself on the right path!

Pray with nature. As you pray with nature, become aware of what seems to be the simplest miracles—a flower, the moon, a stream. Admire it, marvel at it, rejoice in its beauty. It will tell you of the magnificence of God the Creator.

Pray your gratitude. Make thankfulness the centerpiece of all your prayer. At the end of every day, try thanking the Lord for one thing you have never thanked God for before. When we practice gratitude, we become more aware of God's gifts. Then not only our prayer but also our entire lives become filled with amazement and praise.

New Forms of Prayer

- Read and discuss the suggestions listed here. Ask participants which one sounds most appealing to them. Share what styles of prayer you feel most comfortable with or an experience where a form of prayer you thought you'd hate ended up being a positive experience.
- Ask participants if they have any other suggestions for ways to pray that aren't listed in this lesson.

Create a prayer, by yourself or with a partner, that expresses one of the following emotions: **joy, sorrow, thanks, fear.** Use any of the prayer styles above. *If you brought art supplies, let participants know they can use these, too.*

JOURNEY OF FAITH **INQUIRY**

Create a prayer, by yourself or with a partner, that expresses one of the following emotions: JOY, SORROW, THANKS, FEAR. Use any of the prayer styles given.

Of the different forms of prayer described here, which, if any, are you excited (or just willing) to try? Have you found other ways to pray that are especially meaningful for you?

***Journey of Faith for Teens: Inquiry, Q7* (826337)**

The process by which adults are initiated into the Catholic faith throughout the United States is now called the OCIA—the Order of Christian Initiation of Adults. "Order" is a clearer translation of the Latin term for the process formerly known as the RCIA—the Rite of Christian Initiation of Adults. People preparing for baptism and reception into the Church celebrate several rites as part of the order to which those rites belong—an order whose mission is to journey in the faith. The US Conference of Catholic Bishops adopted the name change in 2021, with American dioceses introducing the name thereafter. For more information, please contact your local diocese.

Imprimi Potest: Stephen T. Rehrauer, CSsR, Provincial,
Denver Province, the Redemptorists.

Imprimatur: "In accordance with CIC 827, permission to publish has been granted on March 29, 2016, by the Most Reverend Edward M. Rice, Auxiliary Bishop, Archdiocese of St. Louis. Permission to publish is an indication that nothing contrary to Church teaching is contained in this work. It does not imply any endorsement of the opinions expressed in the publication; nor is any liability assumed by this permission."

Journey of Faith for Teens © 2000, 2016 Liguori Publications, Liguori, MO 63057. All rights reserved. No part of this publication may be reproduced, distributed, stored, transmitted, or posted in any form by any means without prior written permission. To order, visit Liguori.org or call 800-325-9521. Liguori Publications, a nonprofit corporation, is an apostolate of the Redemptorists. To learn more about the Redemptorists, visit Redemptorists.com.

© 2023 Liguori Publications. Photocopying prohibited

Editors of 2016 edition: Theresa Nienaber and Pat Fosarelli, MD, DMin.
Design: Lorena Mitre Jimenez. Images: Shutterstock.

Scripture texts in this work are taken from the *New American Bible*, revised edition ©2010, 1991, 1986, 1970 Confraternity of Christian Doctrine, Washington, D.C., and are used by permission of the copyright owner. All Rights Reserved. No part of the New American Bible may be reproduced in any form without permission in writing from the copyright owner. Excerpts from English translation of the *Catechism of the Catholic Church* for the United States of America © 1994 United States Catholic Conference, Inc. —*Libreria Editrice Vaticana*; English translation of the Catechism of the Catholic Church: Modifications from the Editio Typica © 1997 United States Catholic Conference, Inc. —*Libreria Editrice Vaticana*. Compliant with *The Roman Missal, Third Edition*.

Printed in the United States of America.
Third Edition.

Liguori PUBLICATIONS
A Redemptorist Ministry

Journey of Faith

Journaling

Of the different forms of prayer described in this lesson, which, if any, are you excited (or just willing) to try? Have you found other ways to pray that are especially meaningful for you?

Closing Prayer

Pray spontaneously using the "Pray your gratitude" suggestion found in the lesson. Ask each person to thank the Lord for one thing he or she has never thanked God for before. End your prayer by praying the Lord's Prayer together.

Looking Ahead

Ask participants to pick three new ways to pray and try them out at least once between now and your next lesson.

Q8: Catholic Prayers and Practices

Catechism: 524; 971; 1168–1173; 2759–72

Objectives

- Consider how personal prayer and traditional (or standard) prayers meet the needs of Catholics at different times and in different ways.
- Discover some traditional Catholic prayers.
- Recall the mysteries of the rosary and their connection with Scripture.
- Practice traditional forms of Catholic prayer.

Leader Meditation

Acts 2:42–47

Many people leave the Church and return later because they miss the tradition and the rituals that bond all Catholics to the ancient Church. If you couldn't attend Church, which traditions would you miss the most? Which traditions bind you most closely to God? Which traditions bring you into closest contact with Jesus and his teachings? Meditate on what it means to be Catholic.

Leader Preparation

- Read the lesson, this lesson plan, the Scripture passage, and the *Catechism* sections. Review these related lessons if necessary: Q7, Q14, E4, and E6.
- Consider asking your parish to donate rosaries for your participants and hand them out during class.
- If you have any other sacramentals that mean something to you, bring those in to show your class and encourage sponsors to do the same. *Examples: prayer cards, breviary, rosary, monstrance, holy water, icon, statue, or a scapular.*
- Be familiar with the vocabulary terms for this lesson: hallowed, amen, rosary, monstrance. Definitions are provided in this guide's glossary.

Welcome

Greet participants as they arrive. Check for supplies and immediate needs. Solicit questions or comments about the previous session and/or share new information and findings. Begin promptly.

Opening Scripture

Acts 2:42–47

Ask a volunteer to light the candle and read aloud. Afterward, allow a moment of silence, then welcome comments or reactions. Before beginning your discussion of the lesson handout, ask participants, ***"How does the mission of the early Church guide our Church today? What traditions do we continue today that have their roots in the early Church?"***

> The tradition of Christian prayer is one of the ways in which the tradition of faith takes shape and grows, especially through the contemplation and study of believers....
>
> *CCC* 2650–51, see *Dei Verbum* 8

INQUIRY Q8

In Short:

- We connect to God through personal and traditional prayers.
- The rosary reflects on the mystery of Christ.
- There are many traditional Catholic prayers to try.

Catholic Prayers and Practices

We live in a world filled with nonstop activity, and finding time to pray or talk with God can be just as big a challenge as finding the right words. When you aren't sure where to start, the common prayers Catholics learn can be helpful. Prayers that are memorized or written down also help when we don't know what to say or when we are so upset we can't think clearly. Repeated prayer helps to still our minds and focus our attention on God.

Another big advantage to learning prayers is that it makes it very easy to pray with others. While personal conversation with God is important, community prayer is given the highest regard by Jesus, who assures us that when two or more are gathered in his name, he is there (Matthew 18:20).

The following Catholic prayers are among the most important to Catholics.

The Lord's Prayer

Our Father, who art in heaven, hallowed be thy name; thy kingdom come; thy will be done on earth as it is in heaven. Give us this day our daily bread; and forgive us our trespasses as we forgive those who trespass against us; and lead us not into temptation, but deliver us from evil. Amen (Matthew 6:9–13).

The Lord's Prayer is the prayer Jesus taught his disciples when they asked him how they should pray. We are the adopted daughters and sons of God, and so we can call God "Father." We don't pray for ourselves alone, but for everyone as members of God's family. As children of God, we want to honor God. **Hallowed** means to "make holy"; we want God's name to be honored by all, and we want God's desire for humanity to be fulfilled. All that Jesus did and all that he taught was the will of God. We pray that we may have help and strength to do God's will. And God's will is for us to have life and have life fully.

Spiritually, Christ is our daily bread for the great journey, the food for life which we can receive every day in the Eucharist. In addition to this food, we ask God for all that we need to live each day including forgiveness. We recognize our sinfulness, but we also acknowledge God's merciful love and forgiveness. If we hope for forgiveness from God, we must be willing to forgive others. Finally, we pray to be kept safe from the power of evil and all that leads to evil, because that is what is so damaging to people and to all creation. You'll learn more about the Lord's Prayer later, in *Enlightenment* lesson E6.

TEENS

© 2023 Liguori Publications. Photocopying prohibited

CCC 524; 971; 1168–73; 2759–72

Q8

Catholic Prayers and Practices

- Since participants haven't been instructed in the Mass, petition, or intercession yet, keep the focus on honoring God during this lesson. Explain that the Catholic Church encourages prayers from Scripture, the saints, and the Church because of their closeness to God.
- After reading the introductory text, discuss with participants what these traditional prayers might offer that personal prayer doesn't and vice versa.

Suggested responses include: traditional prayers allow us to pray as a group, unite us with Catholics all over the world, and unite us to our ancestors in faith. Personal prayer helps us build a unique relationship with God and allows us to express our personality in our faith.

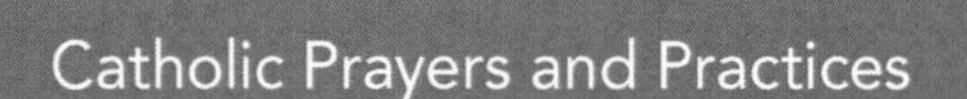

Take time to pray the first four prayers before discussing them. Ask participants to respond to the prayer after you're finished with each section.

INQUIRY

JOURNEY OF FAITH

The Sign of the Cross

1. 2. 3. 4.

In the name of the Father, and of the Son, and of the Holy Spirit. Amen.

This prayer dates to the second century, when Christians would trace the sign of the cross on their foreheads with their thumbs so they could recognize each other during times of persecution.

Today, Catholics traditionally begin and end their prayers with the sign of the cross, which proclaims their faith in the mystery of the Holy Trinity. When we end on amen, we're saying, "yes, we believe" and confirming what comes before it.

The Hail Mary

Hail Mary, full of grace, the Lord is with you; blessed are you among women, and blessed is the fruit of your womb, Jesus. Holy Mary, Mother of God, pray for us sinners now and at the hour of our death. Amen.

Like the Lord's Prayer, the Hail Mary comes directly from Scripture. It begins with the words of the Archangel Gabriel in Luke 1:28 and continues with the words of Mary's cousin Elizabeth in Luke 1:42, "Most blessed are you among women, and blessed is the fruit of your womb." The prayer concludes with our petition that Mary intercede for us, because she is the Mother of God, a woman who lived a life of perfect faithfulness to God.

Doxology

Glory be to the Father, and to the Son, and to the Holy Spirit, as it was in the beginning, is now, and will be forever. Amen.

A **doxology** is a prayer of praise and gratitude to God. Traditionally, Catholics have called this doxology the Glory Be.

The Apostles' Creed

The Apostles' Creed has its roots in an ancient Roman creed. It is a basic statement of Christian beliefs, simpler than the more detailed Nicene Creed used in Catholic liturgy (see Lesson E4 "The Nicene Creed").

I believe in God, the Father almighty, Creator of heaven and earth

There is only one God, whom Jesus instructed us to call our Father. God created everything there is.

and in Jesus Christ, his only Son, our Lord

We believe in Jesus who is God's only Son from all eternity. Jesus is our Master.

who was conceived by the Holy Spirit, born of the Virgin Mary

Jesus' conception was a miracle of the Holy Spirit, since Mary remained a virgin.

suffered under Pontius Pilate, was crucified, died and was buried

The Roman governor Pilate ordered Jesus' execution. Jesus did die and was buried.

he descended into hell; on the third day he rose again from the dead

After he died, but before his resurrection on the Sunday after Good Friday, Jesus went to those people who had died long before him to save them also. This is what the prayer means by "hell."

he ascended into heaven, and is seated at the right hand of God the Father almighty

Jesus returned to heaven to be with his Father.

from there he will come to judge the living and the dead

Jesus will return to judge all people on Judgment Day.

I believe in the Holy Spirit, the holy catholic Church

The Holy Spirit exists. The Church is holy because Jesus is its head; it is catholic (small "c") which means universal or everywhere throughout history.

the communion of saints, the forgiveness of sins,

All of us—the living and the dead—are united in our dedication to God. Furthermore, through God's mercy, our sins are always forgiven.

the resurrection of the body, and life everlasting. Amen

We will all rise one day after we have died with glorified bodies, and we will live forever with God.

The Rosary

The rosary is a meditation on the events (called "mysteries") in the life of Jesus and Mary. There are four sets, each including five mysteries: the Joyful Mysteries, the Sorrowful Mysteries, the Glorious Mysteries, and the Luminous Mysteries.

The rosary is an excellent everyday prayer and is especially useful when we want to pray but find it difficult or impossible to pray in our own words. For many Catholics, the rosary offers great comfort in difficult times.

1. Make the sign of the cross and say the Apostles' Creed.
2. Say the Lord's Prayer.
3. Say three Hail Marys.
4. Say the Glory Be and announce the first mystery.
5. Say the Lord's Prayer.
6. Say ten Hail Marys while meditating on the mystery.
7. Repeat steps 4, 5, and 6, continuing with the second, third, fourth, and fifth mysteries.

Other Catholic Practices

Benediction of the Blessed Sacrament
A benediction is a blessing of the people. Here the people are blessed with the sacred host (the Eucharist is kept in a **monstrance**, a vessel constructed of precious metals in such a way that the consecrated host is clearly visible). The blessing begins with readings from Scripture, hymns, prayers, and silent worship. The Benediction focuses on the mystery of Christ's presence in the Eucharist.

Blessing
This is the placing of a person or object under the care of God or dedicating a person or thing to the service of God. A simple blessing is usually made with the sign of the cross, sometimes along with the sprinkling of holy water. The Church also has a large number of specific blessings for various times and special occasions.

Contemplation
Contemplation is a form of silent, meditative prayer in which a person rests in the knowledge and love of God.

Corporal and Spiritual Works of Mercy
The fourteen works are rooted in the Scriptures. The corporal works of mercy are: feed the hungry, give drink to the thirsty, clothe the naked, visit the imprisoned, shelter the homeless, visit the sick, and bury the dead. The spiritual works of mercy are: counsel the doubtful, instruct the ignorant, admonish sinners, comfort the afflicted, forgive offenses, bear wrongs patiently, pray for the living and the dead.

Fasting and Abstinence
Fasting involves not eating between meals and eating less at regular meals. Fasting is required only on Ash Wednesday (the first day of Lent) and Good Friday for those in good health from ages eighteen through fifty-nine. Abstinence is refraining from eating meat. Abstinence is required on Ash Wednesday, Good Friday, and all the Fridays during Lent for those in good health who are fourteen years old and older.

Genuflection
This is the act of bending down on the right knee while entering a pew or crossing in front of the tabernacle. It is a sign of faith and an act of reverence (respect) for the presence of Jesus Christ in the Eucharist.

Retreat
A retreat is a period of time dedicated to prayer, reflection, and solitude. Its purpose is to deepen our relationship with God.

Sacramentals
These are sacred signs and symbols that help to make our faith more meaningful. Examples of sacramentals include blessed palms, blessed ashes, blessed candles, blessed medals, and holy water.

Q8

The Rosary

- If you have time, discuss the historical background of the rosary. You could also point out how the Luminous Mysteries were added by Pope St. John Paul II.
- If you'd like to and have the time in your class, emphasize the rosary's scriptural nature by showing participants how the rosary has its foundation in Scripture. You can also look online for a scriptural rosary to pray with your group, or order Liguori's pamphlet *Let's Pray (Not Just Say) the Rosary* for each participant.
- Emphasize that Mary and the saints intercede for us to God. We don't worship them but seek their help because they are close to God in heaven.

Other Catholic Practices

- If you brought any sacramentals with you, spend time explaining them to participants and share why they are important to you.
- Allow time for participants to ask questions about the lesson tonight. Much misinformation exists regarding our traditions and beliefs. Don't hesitate to say you don't know the answer to a question. Let the participant know that you will find the answer and follow up later.

As a group, list other prayers or practices you've heard about or observed but don't really understand. If you have time, discuss or research their origin in class. If not, pick one or two to research with your sponsor.

JOURNEY OF FAITH **INQUIRY**

As a group, list any other prayers or practices you've heard about or observed but don't really understand. If you have time, discuss or research their origin in class. If not, pick one or two to research with your sponsor.

Do any of the Catholic prayers discussed in this lesson resonate with you?

Are any of them confusing or intimidating? Why?

***Journey of Faith for Teens: Inquiry*, Q8 (826337)**

The process by which adults are initiated into the Catholic faith throughout the United States is now called the OCIA—the Order of Christian Initiation of Adults. "Order" is a clearer translation of the Latin term for the process formerly known as the RCIA—the Rite of Christian Initiation of Adults. People preparing for baptism and reception into the Church celebrate several rites as part of the order to which those rites belong—an order whose mission is to journey in the faith. The US Conference of Catholic Bishops adopted the name change in 2021, with American dioceses introducing the name thereafter. For more information, please contact your local diocese.

Imprimi Potest: Stephen T. Rehrauer, CSsR, Provincial, Denver Province, the Redemptorists.

Imprimatur: "In accordance with CIC 827, permission to publish has been granted on March 29, 2016, by the Most Reverend Edward M. Rice, Auxiliary Bishop, Archdiocese of St. Louis. Permission to publish is an indication that nothing contrary to Church teaching is contained in this work. It does not imply any endorsement of the opinions expressed in the publication; nor is any liability assumed by this permission."

Journey of Faith for Teens © 2000, 2016 Liguori Publications, Liguori, MO 63057. All rights reserved. No part of this publication may be reproduced, distributed, stored, transmitted, or posted in any form by any means without prior written permission. To order, visit Liguori.org or call 800-325-9521. Liguori Publications, a nonprofit corporation, is an apostolate of the Redemptorists. To learn more about the Redemptorists, visit Redemptorists.com.

© 2023 Liguori Publications. Photocopying prohibited

Editors of 2016 edition: Theresa Nienaber and Pat Fosarelli, MD, DMin. Design: Lorena Mitre Jimenez. Images: Shutterstock.

Scripture texts in this work are taken from the *New American Bible*, revised edition ©2010, 1991, 1986, 1970 Confraternity of Christian Doctrine, Washington, D.C., and are used by permission of the copyright owner. All Rights Reserved. No part of the New American Bible may be reproduced in any form without permission in writing from the copyright owner. Excerpts from English translation of the *Catechism of the Catholic Church* for the United States of America © 1994 United States Catholic Conference, Inc.—*Libreria Editrice Vaticana*; English translation of the Catechism of the Catholic Church: Modifications from the Editio Typica © 1997 United States Catholic Conference, Inc.—*Libreria Editrice Vaticana*. Compliant with *The Roman Missal, Third Edition*.

Printed in the United States of America.
Third Edition.

Journaling

Do any of these Catholic prayers resonate with you? Are any confusing or intimidating? Why?

Closing Prayer

Ask participants to voice any special intentions. Then close with a prayer from the lesson. This might be a good opportunity to pray a decade of the rosary together. Introduce the decade/mystery by reading the corresponding Scripture passage.

Looking Ahead

Traditions like these prayers bind us together with Catholics from any time and place. Why might this kind of unity be important for Catholics? Ask participants to reflect on other ways tradition creates community among believers.

Q9: The Mass

Catechism: 1341–1419

Objectives

- Distinguish between the two parts of the Mass.
- Identify all major actions and events during the Mass by their function and importance.
- Recognize the liturgy as the re-presentation of the paschal mystery.
- Begin to recognize the Real Presence in the Eucharist.

Leader Meditation

Luke 22:14–20

Reflect on the meaning the Mass has for you. Make a renewed effort to really remain focused and connected during Mass next Sunday. When you receive the Body and Blood of our Lord, try to do so with unwavering affirmation that you recognize you are receiving the Real Presence of Jesus Christ.

Leader Preparation

- Read the lesson, this lesson plan, the Scripture passage, and the Catechism sections.
- Be familiar with the vocabulary terms for this lesson: Mass, liturgy, penitential act, *Gloria*, *Lectionary*, responsorial psalm, alleluia, Gospel, homily, petitions, offertory, acclamation, consecration, paschal mystery, Eucharist. Definitions are in this guide's glossary. Additional information and details are available in *The Roman Missal.*
- If possible, make a copy of the petitions from the coming week's Sunday Mass to use as the closing prayer.
- Gather Mass and Mass-reading resources: a copy of *The Roman Missal, Lectionary,* and other materials.
- If possible, gather copies of a simple spiritual-communion prayer for distribution.

Welcome

Greet participants as they arrive. Check for supplies and immediate needs. Solicit questions or comments about the previous session and/or share new information and findings. Begin promptly.

Opening Scripture

Luke 22:14–20

Ask for a volunteer to light the candle and read aloud. Suggest that the participants imagine they are gathered around a table with Jesus and they are actually hearing the words from him. Ask them to picture Jesus sharing the bread and the wine with them personally. Before beginning your discussion of the lesson handout, ask participants, ***"Is there anything in this Scripture passage that reminds you of the Mass?"***

> It was above all on "the first day of the week," Sunday, the day of Jesus' resurrection, that the Christians met "to break bread"....Today we encounter [the celebration of the Eucharist] everywhere in the Church with the same fundamental structure. It remains the center of the Church's life.
>
> *CCC 1343*

INQUIRY Q9

In Short:

- The Mass has two main parts.
- All actions and events of the Mass have a specific function.
- The liturgy is the re-presentation of the paschal mystery.
- Jesus Christ is truly present in the Eucharist.

The Mass

Imagine you are attending a family reunion hosted by your grandparents. They warmly greet family members as they arrive. Each family or individual brings something special to add to this celebration.

It's great to see relatives shake hands and embrace one another, even those who haven't spoken to each other for a long time. For today, differences are forgotten because there is so much to celebrate. Older relatives bring out photographs of loved ones who have died. You meet relatives you never met before and appreciate those you know well even more. You are amazed by the extent of your family and touched by the love that's present.

Why Is the Mass So Important to Catholics?

For Catholics who view their faith communities as part of the family of God, the Mass, especially the Sunday Eucharistic liturgy, is like a special family reunion. It's a time when the children of God gather to give thanks and praise to God, listen to the word of the Lord through sacred Scripture, and be nourished by Christ's Body and Blood in holy Communion. For mature Catholics, Sunday (or Saturday evening) **Mass** isn't just another obligation but a celebration of faith that takes place at the table of the Lord. Individuals alongside the entire community of faith grow and are strengthened by the **liturgy**, a word that means "the participation of the People of God in 'the work of God'" (*CCC* 1069).

Let's briefly examine the principal parts of the Mass.

The Introductory Rites

Mass begins with the gathering of the faith community into a place of worship—usually the parish church. The community of believers is completed by the entrance of the ministers and the priest (also called the presider or celebrant) who will preside over the celebration. A deacon also may assist with the celebration. Often at this time, a gathering hymn is sung by the community, also called the assembly.

The priest leads the assembly in the sign of the cross, reminding us of our faith in the Holy Trinity and of Jesus' victory over death. In doing this, members acknowledge the very Real Presence of Christ in their midst. During the **introductory rites** and throughout the liturgy, the assembly is asked to respond in word and song. The assembly's active participation is very important because that's what gives prayer meaning and life. Through our response, prayer becomes conversation or dialogue with God.

TEENS

© 2023 Liguori Publications. Photocopying prohibited

CCC 1069, 1341–1419

The Mass

- Read the introductory anecdote together, then ask why it's important to get together and celebrate as a family or community. Build on this discussion by asking what that has to do with Mass and the Catholic community.

The Introductory Rites

- After you read about the Penitential Act, pause to discuss the reflection questions as a group. Emphasize how forgiveness is an integral part of any relationship, just like spending time together or coming together to celebrate.

If you have time, you can relate this to the parable of the Prodigal Son in Luke 15:11–32.

The Liturgy of the Word

- Pause after you finish going through this section. Ask participants to think about a Mass they've attended and if these explanations help open up the meaning of these different parts. Encourage participants to think about what they've learned the next time they attend Mass and try to engage with the Liturgy of the Word on an even deeper level.

Next is the **penitential act**, a time when we recall moments when our actions or thoughts separated us from God. Before we can freely and fully participate in this celebration, we must ask God for forgiveness and mercy. In so doing, God washes away the sins that separates us from God—and one another.

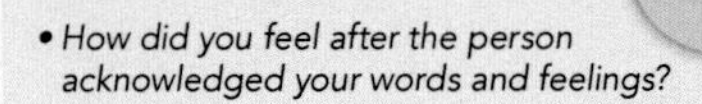

Recall a time when you asked forgiveness from someone.

- *How did you feel after the person acknowledged your words and feelings?*
- *Does asking for—and receiving—forgiveness strengthen relationships? How?*

From the penitential act, we move to the "**Gloria**," or "Glory to God," an ancient hymn of praise that begins with the song of the angels from St. Luke's account of the birth of Christ. The "Gloria" is often sung because of its joyful, powerful words. Then, after a moment of silent prayer, the presider gathers or collects the prayers of the assembly and presents them to God.

The Liturgy of the Word

The **Liturgy of the Word** is a time when God speaks to us through sacred Scripture. These readings are taken from the **Lectionary**, a book containing the Scripture readings for Mass on a given day.

The *Lectionary* is not the same as the Bible, but the *Lectionary* readings are taken from Scripture. Readings are organized by day or theme (baptism, marriage, and so on). An individual *Lectionary* reading is called a *pericopes*, meaning "section" or "cutting" because it is only a portion of a book or chapter of the Bible.

Readings From Scripture

The first reading is usually taken from the Old Testament except during the Easter season. This reading helps us understand the history of our faith by telling us about God's faithful relationship with the ancient Jews, who, because of God's revelation to them, understood themselves to be God's Chosen People. Usually the first reading relates to the day's Gospel reading.

The **responsorial psalm** follows the first reading. The psalms were originally composed as songs to God, so the responsorial psalm is usually sung. It is our response to the Word of the Lord in the first reading—a dialogue with God.

On Sundays and solemnities, a second reading follows the psalm. It is taken from the writings of St. Paul or one of the other Letters of the New Testament. It does not necessarily relate to the other readings but familiarizes us with the lessons taught by these early Christian writers.

The singing of the "**Alleluia**" precedes the third and final reading, called the Gospel (except during Lent when another acclamation is sung). The "Alleluia" emphasizes the presence of Jesus in the word of God. The Gospel is taken from Matthew, Mark, or Luke depending on the year. John's Gospel is read during Advent, Christmas, Lent, and Easter. We stand up during the Gospel as a sign of our reverence and respect because the Gospels contain the words of Jesus himself.

The readings for Sunday liturgies are arranged so that, over the course of three years, almost all of the New Testament and much of the Old Testament is read.

Reflection on the Readings

The homily follows the proclamation of the Gospel. The **homily**, usually given by the presider or sometimes another ordained minister present at the Mass, seeks to explain the day's Scripture readings and make them more meaningful to our lives today. It's important we listen with open minds and hearts.

If we listen with our minds hungry for Christ's vision and direction, there will always be something in the Liturgy of the Word that we can take with us.

The faith community responds to the readings and homily by standing and reciting the Creed, our profession of faith (see E4, "The Creed").

Universal Prayer
With our faith renewed, we present our petitions to God; this time of laying our specific needs before God is also called **Universal Prayer.** We pray for the Church, our world, and our local community.

These petitions bring the Liturgy of the Word to a close. Christ's presence through his word has been made very real to us. We now enter a deep union with Christ and with Catholics throughout the world in the **Liturgy of the Eucharist**—the supper of the Lord.

The Liturgy of the Eucharist

Preparation of the Gifts
During the **offertory**, the bread and wine are brought to the altar to be prepared for offering. In the early Church, members of the faith community brought food and other necessities. Eventually, this became known as the collection, when parishioners make financial contributions toward the care and upkeep of the parish. Special collections for the poor and needy are also taken at this time.

The prayers spoken during the preparation of the gifts thank God for all the gifts we have been given. Then we offer to God our gifts, the work of human hands. The bread and wine that we offer represent a return to God of all we are, and we ask that they be transformed into the bread of life and the cup of salvation.

The Eucharistic Prayer

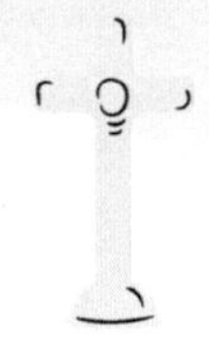

This magnificent prayer begins with a song of praise to God called the "**Holy, Holy, Holy.**" It's usually sung because it's based upon the song of the angels in the Book of Isaiah 6:3. It is proclaimed by the entire assembly.

The priest then asks God to send the Spirit to transform the simple gifts of bread and wine into the Body and Blood of Christ. The prayer recalls and mystically makes present the event of the Last Supper, when Jesus took the bread and wine, gave thanks to God, and transformed them into his Body and Blood (more about this in C5: "The Eucharist"). The moment when the bread and wine are changed into the Body and Blood of our Lord is called the **consecration**. With the words of consecration, Jesus is present as an offering to God to bring us closer to God, despite our imperfections.

The assembly responds with the mystery of faith, also called the paschal mystery. This paschal mystery—Christ's death, rising, and eventual return in glory—is central to our faith.

The Eucharistic Prayer ends with the great "Amen," by which the entire faith community means, "Yes, we believe!" in all that is taking place.

The Communion Rite
This rite begins with the Lord's Prayer, which is recited or sung by the assembly. With the sign of peace, we extend a gesture of our unity in Christ to one another by shaking hands or even hugging.

Then, in the **Eucharist**, we share in the Body and Blood so that, though many in number, we become one body in Christ. In this meal, we are united with every other believer. The Eucharist is our most intimate union with our Lord.

Mass concludes with a brief prayer after the Eucharist and the final blessing. After being nourished at the Lord's table, we are sent forth with the command, "Go forth, the Mass is ended" or "Go in peace, glorifying the Lord by your life." And we respond, "Thanks be to God!"

Preparation of the Gifts

- After reading this section, ask participants why it's important we prepare gifts to offer to God.

You can connect this to their lives by asking how they would "prepare" a gift they'd give to a friend. Would they spend time reflecting on something meaningful before picking the gift out or just pick up the first thing they see? Would they present it to their friend in a meaningful way or hand it to their friend while complaining about what they'd rather be doing?

The Eucharistic Prayer

- Emphasize the importance of the Eucharist as the high point of the Mass and how we share a meal together as believers.

You can continue to connect this to participants' lives by comparing it to a shared meal as the focal point of a family celebration. You can also connect this to Scripture by noting its connection to the Last Supper. If you have time you can read Matthew 26:26–30 aloud.

- Ask participants how they understand Jesus' presence in the Eucharist. Emphasize it is Jesus' *Real* (not symbolic) Presence and that you'll discuss this in more detail in lesson C5: "The Eucharist."

Communion Rite

- When discussing the Communion rite, instruct and encourage participants in making a spiritual communion, providing a prayer if possible. Also model the proper position for receiving a blessing in the Communion line (arms crossed across chest).
- As you wrap up, ask participants if their thoughts on the Mass have changed. End with a discussion on how participating in the Mass strengthens our relationships with God and other Catholics.

Answers to this activity are:

(1) *Hebrew Scripture* or *Old Testament*

(2) *The homily*

(3) *The Creed*

(4) *Isaiah*

(5) *Consecration*

(6) *Unity*

(7) *Presider or deacon*

(8) *Composed as songs* or *psalms to God*

(9) *Stand*

(10) *The mystery of faith* or *paschal mystery*

The first reading is taken from ____________________

____________ follows the reading of the Gospel.

____________________ is our profession of faith.

The "Holy, Holy, Holy" comes from the Book of ____________________ .

The ______________________ is the moment when the bread and wine are changed into the Body and Blood of our Lord.

The sign of peace is a gesture of ____________________

The ______________ or ______________ reads the Gospel.

The psalms were originally ____________________

We ______________ when the Gospel is read.

Christ's death, rising, and eventual return in glory is called the ______________.

Catholics are often asked why they are required to attend Mass on Sundays (or Saturday evenings). Think back to our comparison of the faith community to a family. What happens if a family never takes time to be together? Why do relationships—even relationships between people and God—require the commitment of time?

Journey of Faith for Teens: Inquiry, Q9 (826337)

The process by which adults are initiated into the Catholic faith throughout the United States is now called the OCIA—the Order of Christian Initiation of Adults. "Order" is a clearer translation of the Latin term for the process formerly known as the RCIA—the Rite of Christian Initiation of Adults. People preparing for baptism and reception into the Church celebrate several rites as part of the order to which those rites belong—an order whose mission is to journey in the faith. The US Conference of Catholic Bishops adopted the name change in 2021, with American dioceses introducing the name thereafter. For more information, please contact your local diocese.

Imprimi Potest: Stephen T. Rehrauer, CSsR, Provincial, Denver Province, the Redemptorists.

Imprimatur: "In accordance with CIC 827, permission to publish has been granted on March 29, 2016, by the Most Reverend Edward M. Rice, Auxiliary Bishop, Archdiocese of St. Louis. Permission to publish is an indication that nothing contrary to Church teaching is contained in this work. It does not imply any endorsement of the opinions expressed in the publication; nor is any liability assumed by this permission."

Journey of Faith for Teens © 2000, 2016 Liguori Publications, Liguori, MO 63057. All rights reserved. No part of this publication may be reproduced, distributed, stored, transmitted, or posted in any form by any means without prior written permission. To order, visit Liguori.org or call 800-325-9521. Liguori Publications, a nonprofit corporation, is an apostolate of the Redemptorists. To learn more about the Redemptorists, visit Redemptorists.com.

© 2023 Liguori Publications. Photocopying prohibited

Editors of 2016 edition: Theresa Nienaber and Pat Fosarelli, MD, DMin. Design: Lorena Mitre Jimenez. Images: Shutterstock.

Scripture texts in this work are taken from the *New American Bible*, revised edition ©2010, 1991, 1986, 1970 Confraternity of Christian Doctrine, Washington, D.C., and are used by permission of the copyright owner. All Rights Reserved. No part of the New American Bible may be reproduced in any form without permission in writing from the copyright owner. Excerpts from English translation of the *Catechism of the Catholic Church* for the United States of America © 1994 United States Catholic Conference, Inc. —*Libreria Editrice Vaticana*; English translation of the Catechism of the Catholic Church: Modifications from the Editio Typica © 1997 United States Catholic Conference, Inc. —*Libreria Editrice Vaticana*. Compliant with *The Roman Missal, Third Edition*.

Printed in the United States of America.
Third Edition.

Liguori PUBLICATIONS A Redemptorist Ministry

Journey of Faith

Journaling

Catholics are often asked why they are required to attend Mass on Sundays (or Saturday evenings). Think back to our comparison of the faith community to a family. What happens if a family never takes time to be together? Why do relationships—even relationships between people and God—require the commitment of time?

Closing Prayer

Close with a reading of the petitions. Lead participants in the response, "Lord, hear our prayer." You can also finish with a recitation of the Lord's Prayer, which is prayed at every Mass.

Looking Ahead

This week, have participants think about other ways they get together with their families. Special holiday traditions? Annual reunions or summer trips?

Q10: The Church Year

Catechism: 524–25, 1163–73, 1095, 1194–95

Objectives

- List the seasons of the Church year in the order they occur.
- Indicate which colors, symbols, and themes belong to what Church season.
- Name some feasts, holy days, and major saints celebrated during the liturgical year.
- Consider how individual elements of the Church year combine for a meaningful integration of the life of the Church and the paschal mystery.

Leader Meditation

Ecclesiastes 3:1 and Mark 13:28–29

After reading these Scripture passages, reflect on the liturgical calendar and the framework and structure it offers for the expression of our faith, the sense of rhythm and rightness it brings to Church life, and the channel or passageway it provides for entering into the life, death, and resurrection of Christ for all the faithful.

Leader Preparation

- Read the lesson, this lesson plan, the Scripture passages, and the *Catechism* sections.
- Be familiar with the vocabulary terms for this lesson: liturgical year, Ordinary Time, Lent, Easter Triduum, Easter, feast days, holy days of obligation. Definitions are in this guide's glossary.
- Gather copies of a current liturgical chart or calendar for participants and sponsors. Some parishes, organizations, and groups provide these for free as Advent approaches, and others can be purchased year-round. If Advent is near, also consider providing a Jesse Tree resource.

Welcome

Greet participants as they arrive. Check for supplies and immediate needs. Solicit questions or comments about the previous session and/or share new information and findings. Begin promptly.

Opening Scripture

Ecclesiastes 3:1 and Mark 13:28–29

Ask a volunteer to light the candle and read aloud. Suggest that participants think about patterns in their own lives that provide a rhythm that brings order and structure to school or family life. Before beginning your discussion of the lesson handout, ask participants, ***"What are some signs a particular holiday or season is coming? How does the Church signal a new season is coming?"***

> Once each week, on the day which she [Holy Mother Church] has called the Lord's Day, she keeps the memory of the Lord's resurrection....In the course of the year, moreover, she unfolds the whole mystery of Christ....
>
> CCC 1163

Q10 INQUIRY

In Short:

- The Church follows a liturgical calendar.
- Each liturgical season has its own symbols, themes, and colors.
- The liturgical calendar includes feast days, holy days, and saints days.
- All the liturgical elements combine for a fuller understanding of the paschal mystery.

The Church Year

- *Describe a tradition in your family or close group of friends that is especially important and meaningful to you. Perhaps a Christmas tradition, a birthday tradition, or a summer vacation tradition comes to mind.*
- *Why is this particular tradition important to you? How do traditions help to bind friends and families together?*

The Meaning of Liturgy

The word *liturgy* originally meant "work of the people." Catholic liturgy is "the participation of the People of God in 'the work of God'" (*CCC* 1069). Through the liturgy, Jesus Christ continues in the work of our redemption. Liturgy involves us in the life of the Church and requires the full participation of everyone.

The liturgy in which Catholics participate most often is Sunday Mass, which can also be celebrated on Saturday night. Through our active involvement in the liturgy, we become Christ's body—his hands, arms, eyes, and heart—here on earth. As Christians, we are responsible for proclaiming Christ to the world.

"As a body is one though it has many parts, and all the parts of the body, though many, are one body, so also Christ."

1 Corinthians 12:12

The Liturgical Calendar or Cycle

The **liturgical year** or **Church year** is the Church's way of remembering and celebrating the great events of our salvation through Jesus Christ. Each year follows a pattern, and the readings and prayers for Mass have been organized to fit into it. Like the seasons we experience through nature, the liturgical year has seasons, each with its own special emphasis and traditions.

Advent

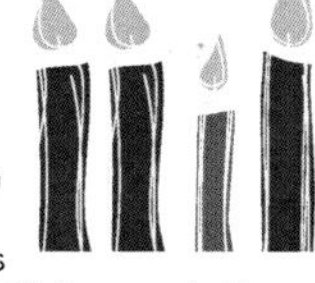

The season of **Advent** marks the beginning of the Church year. Advent is celebrated during the four weeks before Christmas and is a time of anticipation and quiet waiting for the Messiah. The Church invites us to remember that just as Christ grew in his mother's womb some 2,000 years ago, today we must allow him to grow in our hearts. Advent looks to both the past, Christ's birth in the town of Bethlehem, and the future, the unknown time when Christ will come again.

TEENS

© 2023 Liguori Publications. Photocopying prohibited

CCC 524–525, 1163–1173, 1095, 1194–95

The Church Year

- Give participants time to reflect on the introductory questions. Invite them to share with the group.

The Liturgical Calendar or Cycle

- Explain the liturgical year and give participants time to get familiar with the liturgical calendar. Ask participants to list what they notice at first glance. (Make sure you point out the colors, major Church seasons and how to find feast days and holidays.) Ask them to look up the feast day of a favorite saint, or what is celebrated on their birthday. Ask them to find major holidays or seasons.
- Before reading about each liturgical season, have participants find it on the liturgical calendar and list when it begins and ends.
- Pause after each liturgical season and ask participants to list any major symbols or traditions they associate with it. Share a list of symbols and traditions usually associated with these Catholic seasons. *Suggestions are listed below.*

Advent: *the Advent wreath, Nativity scenes, the colors purple and pink, Christmas trees, the star to represent the star of Bethlehem, Christmas carols, additional prayer services focused on anticipation.*

Christmas: *Baby Jesus appears in the Nativity scene, the Three Wise Men (Epiphany), angels, the Holy Spirit (Jesus' baptism), Mary (solemnity of Mary).*

Lent: *the color purple or violet, ashes, palms, the cross, the desert, penance and reconciliation takes on a special meaning, fasting, prayer, almsgiving.*

Easter: *the cross, the empty tomb, lilies, the Holy Spirit (Pentecost).*

Advent

- If there's time and Advent is approaching, present or distribute a Jesse tree, explaining the various symbols and biblical figures and their role in salvation history.

Easter

- Review the date for Easter, reminding participants that they will enter the Church on the night before.

INQUIRY

JOURNEY OF FAITH

Christmas

December 25, the feast of the birth of Christ, marks the beginning of the **Christmas** season. The Christmas season includes the solemnity of Mary the Mother of God on January 1, the feast of the Holy Family on the first Sunday after Christmas, and the feast of the Epiphany. While we may think of the Epiphany as being the discovery of the Christ Child by the three wise men, its real meaning is that Christ comes for the salvation of everyone. The celebration of the Baptism of the Lord, usually the third Sunday after Christmas, ends the Christmas season.

Ordinary Time

Ordinary Time is that time in the yearly cycle that falls outside the other seasons. During Ordinary Time, the mystery of Christ in all its fullness is reflected upon and celebrated. This makes it a time of growth both for us as individuals and for our entire faith community.

Lent

The season of **Lent** begins with Ash Wednesday. Lent is a penitential season, meaning we focus on prayer, fasting, and almsgiving. We perform acts of charity and self-denial to improve and purify our lives in preparation for the celebration of Easter.

Lent lasts forty days, modeled after Jesus' forty days in the desert, as told in the Gospel of Matthew 4:1–11. Lent ends at the Mass of the Lord's Supper, which is part of Holy Week. **Holy Week** is the week beginning with Palm Sunday leading up to Easter Sunday. Holy Week also includes the Easter Triduum.

Easter Triduum

The Easter **Triduum** is a three-day celebration. Holy Thursday recalls the Last Supper and Jesus' first celebration of the holy Eucharist. As an important part of the Last Supper, the liturgy of this evening emphasizes Jesus' command to wash one another's feet, meaning we must serve one another.

Q10

Good Friday recalls the suffering and death of Jesus.

Holy Saturday is a day of prayer and reflection. At sundown, the Easter Vigil begins and the Church bursts into joy and celebrates the resurrection of Jesus. This is the night when the Church traditionally welcomes new members who then receive the sacraments of initiation—baptism (if they have not yet been baptized in a Christian church), confirmation, and holy Eucharist.

Easter

Unlike Christmas, which occurs on the same day every year, Easter is a movable feast. This means the Sunday we celebrate Easter changes each year. As a way to keep the celebration of Easter consistent among new Christians of different cultures and calendars, it was determined that Easter would be celebrated the Sunday after the paschal full moon, which is the first full moon on or after the spring equinox, March 21. This means Easter can fall between March 22 and April 25. **Easter** morning begins the fifty-day period of celebrating the resurrection of Jesus called the Easter season. It concludes with the important feast of Pentecost, the birthday of the Church, which celebrates the coming of the Holy Spirit who fills us, like the first disciples, with the power to bring Jesus to the world.

Ordinary Time

The Easter season is followed by a long period of Ordinary Time that ends just before Advent with the feast of Christ the King. This brings us full circle in our celebration of the liturgical year.

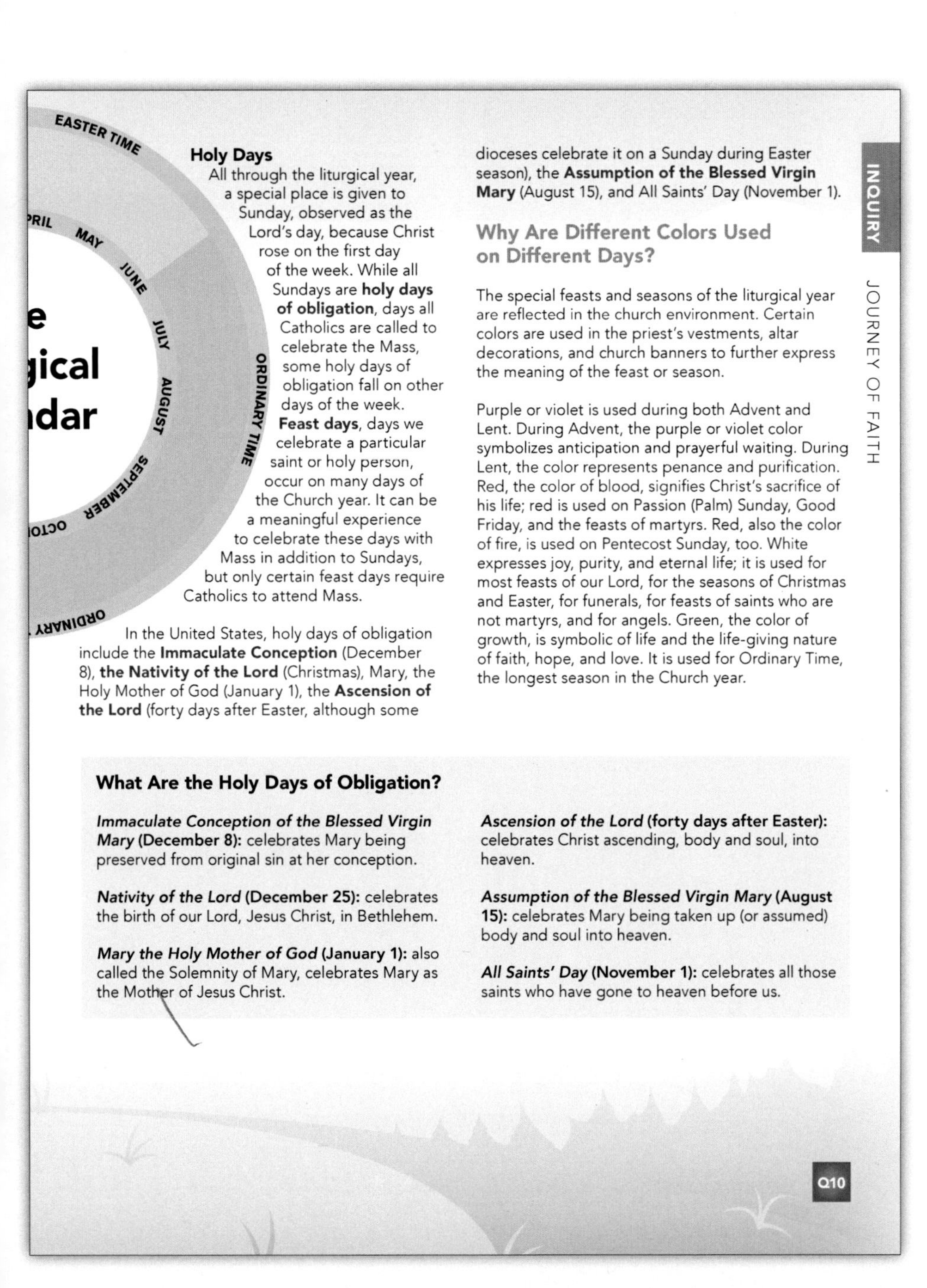

Holy Days

All through the liturgical year, a special place is given to Sunday, observed as the Lord's day, because Christ rose on the first day of the week. While all Sundays are **holy days of obligation**, days all Catholics are called to celebrate the Mass, some holy days of obligation fall on other days of the week. **Feast days**, days we celebrate a particular saint or holy person, occur on many days of the Church year. It can be a meaningful experience to celebrate these days with Mass in addition to Sundays, but only certain feast days require Catholics to attend Mass.

In the United States, holy days of obligation include the **Immaculate Conception** (December 8), **the Nativity of the Lord** (Christmas), Mary, the Holy Mother of God (January 1), the **Ascension of the Lord** (forty days after Easter, although some dioceses celebrate it on a Sunday during Easter season), the **Assumption of the Blessed Virgin Mary** (August 15), and All Saints' Day (November 1).

Why Are Different Colors Used on Different Days?

The special feasts and seasons of the liturgical year are reflected in the church environment. Certain colors are used in the priest's vestments, altar decorations, and church banners to further express the meaning of the feast or season.

Purple or violet is used during both Advent and Lent. During Advent, the purple or violet color symbolizes anticipation and prayerful waiting. During Lent, the color represents penance and purification. Red, the color of blood, signifies Christ's sacrifice of his life; red is used on Passion (Palm) Sunday, Good Friday, and the feasts of martyrs. Red, also the color of fire, is used on Pentecost Sunday, too. White expresses joy, purity, and eternal life; it is used for most feasts of our Lord, for the seasons of Christmas and Easter, for funerals, for feasts of saints who are not martyrs, and for angels. Green, the color of growth, is symbolic of life and the life-giving nature of faith, hope, and love. It is used for Ordinary Time, the longest season in the Church year.

INQUIRY

JOURNEY OF FAITH

What Are the Holy Days of Obligation?

***Immaculate Conception of the Blessed Virgin Mary* (December 8):** celebrates Mary being preserved from original sin at her conception.

***Nativity of the Lord* (December 25):** celebrates the birth of our Lord, Jesus Christ, in Bethlehem.

***Mary the Holy Mother of God* (January 1):** also called the Solemnity of Mary, celebrates Mary as the Mother of Jesus Christ.

***Ascension of the Lord* (forty days after Easter):** celebrates Christ ascending, body and soul, into heaven.

***Assumption of the Blessed Virgin Mary* (August 15):** celebrates Mary being taken up (or assumed) body and soul into heaven.

***All Saints' Day* (November 1):** celebrates all those saints who have gone to heaven before us.

Q10

Holy Days

- Discuss why we celebrate special holidays, holy days, solemnities, and memorials in addition to Sunday Mass.

Note the connection between various feasts—for instance, how the annunciation (March 25) is exactly nine months before Christmas.

- If you have time, brainstorm with participants ways they could celebrate a saint's feast day. You can pick a saint for the group or let participants get into groups and choose a saint that means something to them.

Some examples include making a culturally or historically themed meal, planning a culturally or historically themed activity, reading a short biography or writing of the saint, doing an act of service that is somehow connected to the life of the saint, etc.

- Emphasize Holy Days of Obligation aren't about the obligation, but an opportunity to come together as a community of faith. Connect this to participants lives through how families come together in times of great joy (weddings or baby showers) and great sorrow (funerals or serious illness).

Q10

As a group or with a partner, create a chart, list, or other visual showing what colors, symbols, and traditions are associated with which Church seasons. Then list when during the year these seasons take place. Use your liturgical calendar.

JOURNEY OF FAITH | INQUIRY

As a group or with a partner, create a chart, list, or other visual showing what colors, symbols, and traditions are associated with which Church seasons. Then list when during the year these seasons take place. Use your liturgical calendar.

How do Church traditions help to build closeness and community within the people of God?

Of the Catholic practices or traditions you have observed thus far, which holds the most meaning for you? Why?

Journey of Faith for Teens: Inquiry, Q10 (826337)

The process by which adults are initiated into the Catholic faith throughout the United States is now called the OCIA—the Order of Christian Initiation of Adults. "Order" is a clearer translation of the Latin term for the process formerly known as the RCIA—the Rite of Christian Initiation of Adults. People preparing for baptism and reception into the Church celebrate several rites as part of the order to which those rites belong—an order whose mission is to journey in the faith. The US Conference of Catholic Bishops adopted the name change in 2021, with American dioceses introducing the name thereafter. For more information, please contact your local diocese.

Imprimi Potest: Stephen T. Rehrauer, CSsR, Provincial, Denver Province, the Redemptorists.

Imprimatur: "In accordance with CIC 827, permission to publish has been granted on March 29, 2016, by the Most Reverend Edward M. Rice, Auxiliary Bishop, Archdiocese of St. Louis. Permission to publish is an indication that nothing contrary to Church teaching is contained in this work. It does not imply any endorsement of the opinions expressed in the publication; nor is any liability assumed by this permission."

Journey of Faith for Teens © 2000, 2016 Liguori Publications, Liguori, MO 63057. All rights reserved. No part of this publication may be reproduced, distributed, stored, transmitted, or posted in any form by any means without prior written permission. To order, visit Liguori.org or call 800-325-9521. Liguori Publications, a nonprofit corporation, is an apostolate of the Redemptorists. To learn more about the Redemptorists, visit Redemptorists.com.

© 2023 Liguori Publications. Photocopying prohibited

Editors of 2016 edition: Theresa Nienaber and Pat Fosarelli, MD, DMin. Design: Lorena Mitre Jimenez. Images: Shutterstock.

Scripture texts in this work are taken from the *New American Bible*, revised edition ©2010, 1991, 1986, 1970 Confraternity of Christian Doctrine, Washington, D.C., and are used by permission of the copyright owner. All Rights Reserved. No part of the New American Bible may be reproduced in any form without permission in writing from the copyright owner. Excerpts from English translation of the *Catechism of the Catholic Church* for the United States of America © 1994 United States Catholic Conference, Inc. —*Libreria Editrice Vaticana*; English translation of the Catechism of the Catholic Church: Modifications from the Editio Typica © 1997 United States Catholic Conference, Inc. —*Libreria Editrice Vaticana*. Compliant with *The Roman Missal, Third Edition*.

Printed in the United States of America.
Third Edition.

Journaling

How do Church traditions help to build closeness and community within the People of God? Of the Catholic practices or traditions you have observed thus far, which holds the most meaning for you? Why?

Closing Prayer

Close with a spontaneous prayer thanking God for the gift of the Church Year (liturgical calendar), which unites the Church and deepens our faith, just as family gatherings and traditions become a bond among the members.

Looking Ahead

Just as we have traditions that bring us together as a community, we also have special signs or objects that become a part of these traditions. Before the next class, ask participants to spend some time thinking about any special objects that have become a part of your family's traditions.

Q11: Places in a Catholic Church

Catechism: 1179–86, 2179

Objectives

- Locate various places and objects within a typical parish church.
- Describe the various places and objects by function and significance.
- When we gather together in church, Christ is in our midst.

Leader Meditation

Psalm 84

Take your Bible to church when no formal rites are in progress, and kneel silently before the Lord for a few moments. Pray for the guidance and insight you need to instruct the young people in your care. Be aware of the different elements in the church. Meditate on the many ways these symbols have touched your life.

Leader Preparation

- Read the lesson, this lesson plan, the Scripture passage, and the *Catechism* sections.
- Ask the pastor or deacon to assist you in displaying the various vestments to the participants. If he isn't available, simply borrowing a few items will suffice.
- Schedule a tour of a church, sacristy, or chapel. Whether or not this replaces the formal session, provide participants with quiet time for prayer. If a group tour isn't available, encourage participants and sponsors to plan their own private visit to the church.
- Research the histories and missions of your parish. Consider gathering a list of websites and other relevant information for participants and sponsors interested in researching it further.
- Be familiar with the vocabulary terms for this lesson: holy water, sanctuary, altar, *The Roman Missal*, lectern, ambo, tabernacle, crucifix, Easter candle, Stations of the Cross, sacristy, vestments, confessionals, vestibule, rectory, diocese. Definitions are in this guide's glossary.

Welcome

Greet participants as they arrive. Check for supplies and immediate needs. Solicit questions or comments about the previous session and/or share new information and findings. Begin promptly.

Opening Scripture

Psalm 84

If it's possible for this lesson, read aloud from the lectern. Talk about praying in church, the dwelling place of the Lord. Before beginning your discussion of the lesson handout, ask participants to think about, ***"How does the church building you're in now reflect the dwelling place of God talked about in the psalm?"***

Our visible churches, holy places, are images of the holy city, the heavenly Jerusalem toward which we are making our way on pilgrimage.

CCC 1198

Q11 INQUIRY

In Short:

- Everything in the church carries meaning.
- Sacred objects hold significance for Catholics.
- When we gather in church, Christ is there.

Places in a Catholic Church

- *Do you have a special place you consider holy—a place where you can really feel the presence of God? Perhaps it's a place that makes you feel at peace or a place where you feel safe and comfortable. Briefly describe your holy place.*

Catholics have many places they feel they can go to encounter God, but the place most important to Catholic worship is the building we call the parish church. A **parish** church usually has territorial boundaries, meaning it serves a specific geographic area or neighborhood. A few parishes do not have boundaries but were built to serve Catholics with specific needs, such as groups of immigrants who speak languages other than English.

Catholic churches are named in honor of one or all persons of the Trinity, the Virgin Mary, one of the saints, or events that are important to our faith (such as the Assumption or the Nativity).

- *Who was your parish dedicated to? Do you know why?*

Let's look inside a parish church

The first time you step inside a Catholic church, it's natural to feel a little confused or overwhelmed if you are unfamiliar with the symbols. The Church has a rich tradition of using art and symbols (we call this liturgical art) to sanctify the worship space. Everywhere you look in the parish church, there are reminders of God.

When you walk in the door, you will see a bowl of water near the door or a **baptismal font** (1) near the church entrance. These contain **holy water** (2), blessed water used by Catholics to make the sign of the cross as a reminder of their baptism and used in blessings as a sign of God's loving care. The tradition of blessing oneself upon entering the church began centuries ago when basins were kept at the entrances of people's homes and at special places of worship. Visitors would wash their hands and faces before entering another's home or a sacred place. This symbolic cleansing is still with us today.

The **sanctuary** (3) is the area in the front or near the center of the church where the altar, lectern, tabernacle, and sometimes baptismal font are located.

The **altar** (4) is the central table on which the Communion bread and the cup of wine are offered. The book of Mass prayers, called the **Roman Missal** (5), is also used at the altar. Altars are made of precious materials such as stone, marble, or fine wood. The altar itself is a symbol of Christ. Candles on the altar symbolize Christ's presence and light.

TEENS

© 2023 Liguori Publications. Photocopying prohibited

CCC 1179–1186, 2179

Places in a Catholic Church

- After participants reflect on the opening question ask volunteers to share their "holy places." Discuss why the church is a special place for prayer. *(Be sure to mention the Eucharist, altar, tabernacle, and baptismal font or holy water.)*
- Ask if participants know the history behind your parish's name. If no one knows, explain the name and why it's significant.

Let's Look Inside a Parish Church

- If you are inside your parish church, talk about each place and object in the church as the group stands around it. This will require the group to move around.
  If you can't have your lesson in the church, try to have images as a visual aid.
- Discuss how some of these objects—like the crucifix, holy water, or images of the saints—play a role in the lives of Catholics outside the church.

This would also be a good time to direct participants to the sidebar "Why Do Catholics Have a Crucifix?"

Emphasize that while Catholic churches may be filled with images, Catholics don't worship these images. Rather, these images are meant to be reminders and inspiration for Catholics as we strive to live like the saints and imitate Christ, as well as reminders of Christ's suffering and love for us. (Reference *CCC* 1159–62 and 2129–32.)

If you have Stations of the Cross in your church, let participants know that these images are used for prayer and devotion. Tell participants that they will practice the stations during Lent (in lesson E5 "The Way of the Cross"). If you have time, walk through each station and mention the event depicted.

The **ambo** (6) is the place where the word of God is proclaimed to the assembly during Mass and at other services. The book used for these Scripture readings is called the *Lectionary*. All nonscriptural reading and song-leading happens from the **lectern** (7).

The **tabernacle** (8) is a special place where the consecrated Eucharist (the body of Christ in the form of hosts) is kept. Near the tabernacle the **sanctuary lamp** (9) burns continually, reminding us of Jesus' presence in the Eucharist that is reserved, or kept, there.

In older churches, the baptismal font may be in an area in the rear of the church. In newer churches, it is usually in or near the sanctuary. In churches where baptism is performed by immersion (when a person's entire body is submerged in the water), the pool is often located at the church entrance so that all who enter the church are reminded of and can actually renew their baptismal vows as they make the sign of cross with the holy water.

The church sanctuary also contains a **crucifix** (10)—a cross with the image of Jesus on it—representing his suffering and death. Usually the crucifix is permanently hung in a prominent place near the altar. Or it may be brought in during the procession at the beginning of Mass and ritually placed in the sanctuary.

Why do Catholics have a Crucifix?

The Catholic practice of honoring, or venerating, the crucifix is a declaration of our faith in the complete love of God that was shown to us in the death of Jesus Christ.

The image of the crucifix is a symbol of Christ's victory over death and a reminder of his suffering. When looking upon the crucifix, Catholics should be drawn to reverence Christ and thank him for sacrificing himself for our sins. While not all Christian churches use the symbol of the crucifix, many use a cross as a reminder of our salvation through Jesus.

Another very important symbol found in the Catholic Church is the **Easter (paschal) candle** (11). The Easter candle is a large decorated white candle, symbolic of the risen Christ. It is blessed and lighted during the annual Easter Vigil liturgy (held in the late evening on Holy Saturday, the day before Easter Sunday). It is placed near the altar, baptismal font, or pulpit.

Q11

Things and Places in a Catholic Church

1. Baptismal font 2. Holy water 3. Sanctuary 4. Altar 9. Sanctuary lamp 10. Crucifix 11. Easter (paschal) candl

During the Easter season (the weeks following Easter), the Easter candle burns at every liturgy. During the rest of the liturgical year, it is placed near the baptismal font to symbolize our entering into the death and resurrection of Christ at our baptism. At Catholic burial services, the Easter candle is positioned near the casket to symbolize the deceased person's new life with the risen Christ.

Often the sanctuary and worship space of a church are adorned with liturgical art such as banners and tapestries that contain the symbols and colors of the particular liturgical season (Advent, Christmas, Ordinary Time, Lent, and Easter). Sundays and special feast days usually include the use of flowers or other greenery that help us to connect the seasons of the Church year with the seasons of God's magnificent creation.

Churches also have the **Stations of the Cross** (12), a series of fourteen pictures, carvings, or plaques representing events in the suffering and death of Jesus. These are used for prayer and meditation, especially during the season of Lent. The Stations of the Cross are usually found along the inside walls of the church.

Some churches, especially older churches, contain rows of small votive candles. People who offer special prayers of thanksgiving or of petition (asking) light

5. Roman Missal 6. Ambo 7. Lectern 8. Tabernacle
e 12. Stations of the cross 13. Sacristy

candles as a physical representation of those prayers. The burning of the wick in a votive candle and the rise of smoke symbolize our prayers rising to heaven.

What are the other rooms in a church?
The priests and other church ministers prepare for Mass and other services in a room called the **sacristy** (13). The sacristy is usually located behind or off to the side of the sanctuary. This is where priests and deacons put on their **vestments**, the symbolic garments worn during liturgical celebrations.

These vestments include an **alb** and a stole. An alb is a long white garment symbolic of the purity one should have when approaching God and is worn by priests, deacons, and altar servers. The **stole** is a band or sash worn by priests and deacons; deacons wear it diagonally across one shoulder whereas a priest wears it either crossed in front or down both shoulders. The priest's outer garment is called a **chasuble**, and the deacon's is a **dalmatic**. Other ministers might also prepare for Mass in the sacristy, including the lector (reader) and the acolytes (altar servers).

Churches also have **confessionals**, small rooms in which people can celebrate the sacrament of reconciliation or where they can seek advice and counsel from a priest. The confessional is a precious reminder of God's infinite mercy and loving forgiveness.

Many churches have a large gathering space, called the **vestibule**, located just before the entrance into the worship area of the church. This space is an area where parishioners gather together for fellowship and community-building before and after liturgical celebrations.

What are the other buildings near the parish church?
The parish center is a building or large room where parish activities are held. The **rectory** is the place where the parish priests live and work. There may also be a **convent** near your parish church, a place where religious sisters live.

What is the difference between a church and a cathedral?

A cathedral is the official church of the bishop of a diocese. A **diocese** is a geographical area composed of many parishes under the leadership and pastoral care of a bishop.

The cathedral church of the pope, the bishop of Rome, is the basilica of St. John Lateran. St. John Lateran is considered more important than any other church, even St. Peter's in Vatican City.

Vatican City is a 108-acre area in Rome that is the worldwide headquarters of the Catholic Church and the official home of the pope. Vatican City is a recognized state and has diplomatic relations (ongoing discussions among government officials) with many other countries.

No matter what your parish church looks like, it is the heart of your own faith community, the sacred space most important to you. While a beautiful park or your own bedroom can be a holy place for you, at church you come together with the people of God to give thanks and praise to our Lord. The church is a place where believers are called to gather together and celebrate just like you would gather at someone's house or a restaurant to celebrate the holidays or a special family event. Jesus himself emphasized the importance of the Christian faith community when he said, "For where two or three are gathered together in my name, there am I in the midst of them" (Matthew 18:20).

What Are the Other Rooms in a Church?

- If you're able, take participants on a tour of the sacristy and confessionals. If you're unable to get into these spaces, try to have pictures for your lesson. If your parish priest or deacon is able to join you for this part of the lesson, let him lead the discussion and answer any participant questions.

What Are the Other Buildings Near the Parish Church?

- If possible, walk the parish grounds and point out any other buildings central to the life of the parish community (rectory, parish office, school, convent, and so on).
- Return to the church or your regular meeting space and ask participants for any questions. Clarify or explain as you're able. If you don't have an answer, find out for your next meeting.

With a partner or by yourself, look around your parish church and find one or two of the things listed in this lesson and one or two that were not. Write down where they're located in your church, what they look like, and what they symbolize (ask if you don't know). Share with your class to create a master list.

JOURNEY OF FAITH | INQUIRY

With a partner or by yourself, look around your parish church and find one or two of the things listed in this lesson and one or two that were not. Write down where they're located in your church, what they look like, and what they symbolize. If you don't know, ask! Share your findings with your class to create a master list.

Of all the sacred and symbolic objects Catholics use, which ones are you most attracted to? Why?

If you can, try to incorporate these objects into your personal space at home.

Journey of Faith for Teens: Inquiry, Q11 (826337)

The process by which adults are initiated into the Catholic faith throughout the United States is now called the OCIA—the Order of Christian Initiation of Adults. "Order" is a clearer translation of the Latin term for the process formerly known as the RCIA—the Rite of Christian Initiation of Adults. People preparing for baptism and reception into the Church celebrate several rites as part of the order to which those rites belong—an order whose mission is to journey in the faith. The US Conference of Catholic Bishops adopted the name change in 2021, with American dioceses introducing the name thereafter. For more information, please contact your local diocese.

Imprimi Potest: Stephen T. Rehrauer, CSsR, Provincial, Denver Province, the Redemptorists.

Imprimatur: "In accordance with CIC 827, permission to publish has been granted on March 29, 2016, by the Most Reverend Edward M. Rice, Auxiliary Bishop, Archdiocese of St. Louis. Permission to publish is an indication that nothing contrary to Church teaching is contained in this work. It does not imply any endorsement of the opinions expressed in the publication; nor is any liability assumed by this permission."

Journey of Faith for Teens © 2000, 2016 Liguori Publications, Liguori, MO 63057. All rights reserved. No part of this publication may be reproduced, distributed, stored, transmitted, or posted in any form by any means without prior written permission. To order, visit Liguori.org or call 800-325-9521. Liguori Publications, a nonprofit corporation, is an apostolate of the Redemptorists. To learn more about the Redemptorists, visit Redemptorists.com.

© 2023 Liguori Publications. Photocopying prohibited

Editors of 2016 edition: Theresa Nienaber and Pat Fosarelli, MD, DMin. Design: Lorena Mitre Jimenez. Images: Shutterstock.

Scripture texts in this work are taken from the *New American Bible*, revised edition ©2010, 1991, 1986, 1970 Confraternity of Christian Doctrine, Washington, D.C., and are used by permission of the copyright owner. All Rights Reserved. No part of the New American Bible may be reproduced in any form without permission in writing from the copyright owner. Excerpts from English translation of the *Catechism of the Catholic Church* for the United States of America © 1994 United States Catholic Conference, Inc. —*Libreria Editrice Vaticana*; English translation of the Catechism of the Catholic Church: Modifications from the Editio Typica © 1997 United States Catholic Conference, Inc. —*Libreria Editrice Vaticana*. Compliant with *The Roman Missal, Third Edition*.

Printed in the United States of America.
Third Edition.

Liguori PUBLICATIONS
A Redemptorist Ministry

Journey of Faith

Journaling

Of all the sacred and symbolic objects Catholics use, which ones are you most attracted to? Why? If you can, try to incorporate these objects into your personal space at home.

Closing Prayer

Ask for any special intentions and then pray together:

Lord, you have created us to know you, love you, and serve you. Indeed, we are wonderfully made. Thank you for the gift of this church and for the objects and symbols we encounter here that bring us closer to you. Amen.

Looking Ahead

All the places and objects in the church serve different functions. In the same way, each member of the Church plays a unique role in building the Church on earth. Ask participants to think about some of these roles they know of or have heard about and how they help build the Church on earth.

Q12: Who Shepherds the Church?

Catechism: 871–945

Objectives:

- List the levels of authority and jurisdiction within the Catholic hierarchy.
- Describe the institutional Church as founded in Jesus Christ.
- Discover the significance of apostolic succession and Church unity.
- Identify the current pope, the first pope, Peter, and recognize the pope as the shepherd of the Church.
- Recognize that religious orders bring unique ministries and values to the Church.

Leader Meditation

Matthew 16:18–19

Read the passage, then reflect on its meaning with this prayer:

Lord, you have called me to this special purpose, to make your ways known to the young people in your flock. Help me to inspire in them a love for your Church, an obedience to your teachings, an understanding of their own call to serve, and a listening ear to those who have been chosen to lead them. Renew my respect for each member of your Church, clergy and lay. Clarify for me the importance of structure and leadership. I ask this in the name of your Son, Jesus, who stands forever as the head of your body, the Church. Amen.

Leader Preparation

- Read the lesson, this lesson plan, the Scripture passage, and *Catechism* sections.
- Invite your pastor or parish ministry leaders to talk to participants about their roles in the parish. If you haven't already, gather names and contact information for various parish ministries and make these resources available to participants.
- Be familiar with the vocabulary terms for this lesson: pope, Church hierarchy, laity, conclave, Holy See, infallible, ordination, bishop, auxiliary bishop, archdiocese, archbishop, cardinal, diocesan priest, religious priest, pastor, associate pastor, transitional deacon, permanent deacon, religious orders, sister, nun, brother, monk, lector, cantor. Definitions are in this guide's glossary.

Welcome

Greet participants as they arrive. Check for supplies and immediate needs. Solicit questions or comments about the previous session and/or share new information and findings. Begin promptly.

Opening Scripture

Matthew 16:13–20

Ask a volunteer to light the candle and read aloud. Encourage discussion of Jesus' commissioning Peter as the rock of his church. Before beginning your discussion of the lesson handout, ask participants, ***"What do you think it means that Peter is the rock upon which Christ will build his church? What might this mean for the Church today?"***

> In the Church there is diversity of ministry but unity of mission. To the apostles and their successors Christ has entrusted the office of teaching, sanctifying, and governing in his name and by his power.
>
> CCC 873, see Decree on the Apostolate of the Laity, *Apostolicam Actuositatem*, 2

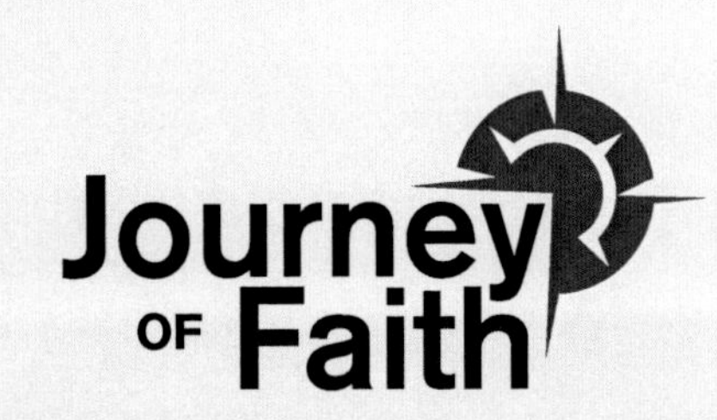

Q12 INQUIRY

In Short:

- The Church was founded by Jesus Christ.
- Apostolic succession works to unite the Church.
- The pope is the shepherd of the Church on earth.

Who Shepherds the Church?

Think about a club, sports team, or band you're a member of; you can even think about your family. All of these things probably have some kind of organization that keeps it running. Your club probably has a president. Your team probably has a coach, and your band has a director. Even in your family everyone has responsibilities to make sure chores get done.

- *Why do organizations need some kind of structure and leadership?*
- *Give an example of good leadership in a group you've been a part of. Why was a good leader important?*
- *Are dedicated members just as important as group leaders? Why or why not?*

Every organization needs someone to take the lead, and every member of that organization has responsibilities unique to his or her talents and capabilities.

Our faith community could not exist without structure or Church leaders, we call this structure the **Church hierarchy**. This lesson introduces you to the structure of the Catholic Church. It also takes a brief look at the people in the Church. From layperson to pope, we all have a role that's important to the life of the Church. The descriptions here are very brief, but you'll learn more as you meet some of these people in your parish and read more about them in your studies.

The Pope

Christ is the head of the Church, what we call the body of Christ. Before ascending to heaven, Jesus gave his disciples special roles and authority in order to continue his mission on earth. Catholics believe these roles and authority have been passed down through the centuries.

In particular, Jesus gave his Apostle Peter the responsibility to lead the whole Church, saying, "You are Peter, and upon this rock I will build my church" (Matthew 16:18). The **pope**, as bishop of Rome, is regarded as Peter's successor, the rock on which the Church is built. Because this is such a great responsibility, cardinals choose the pope with great care. When it's time to select a new pope, the cardinals of the world go to Rome and meet in a **conclave** to prayerfully vote on the man who will become pope.

The pope is the official leader of the Catholic Church on earth. With the help of the bishops of the world, the pope works to spread the teachings of Jesus as they are revealed in Scripture, the traditions of the Church, and our ongoing discovery of the nature of God as God reveals it to us, which we call divine revelation. Just as important as the pope's role as Church leader is his role as servant of the whole Church. The Gospels tell us that Jesus, while leading his followers to God, continually fed them, cured them, taught them—and even washed their feet!

TEENS

© 2023 Liguori Publications. Photocopying prohibited

CCC 871–945

Who Shepherds the Church

- After reading the lesson introduction, talk about the importance of having structure and leadership within organizations. Ask participants to share responses to the lesson questions.
- Relate the needs of the Church to those of other organizations. Emphasize the importance of the laity as the base of the Church organization.

Suggested responses include: leadership, rules and guidelines, and active and dedicated members.

The Pope

- Consider sharing and exploring a list of the Catholic popes from St. Peter through today. Doing so will illustrate the unbroken line of apostolic succession. Highlight the first few, some recent popes, and notable names in between.
- As you discuss the pope, ask participants to identify who the current pope is and try to list some of the pope's responsibilities to the Church.

Suggested responses include: leads the Church, writes encyclicals that clarify and strengthen Church teachings and beliefs, promotes Catholic teachings in the world by addressing poverty and injustices, protects and promotes unity in the Gospel.

- Discuss the sidebar "Can the Pope Make a Mistake?" as a group. *You may also want to mention that we have to be careful when reading or listening to media representations of the pope and his speeches, as it's easy to take things out of context.*

The Bishops

- As you discuss bishops, ask participants to identify any current bishops or archbishops. Make sure you name the bishops and archbishop in your diocese. Then list some of a bishop's responsibilities to the Church.

Suggested responses include: oversees Church life, cardinals vote in the election of a new pope, and ordains priests.

Priests

- As you discuss priests, ask participants to identify the priests who serve your parish. Make sure to identify the pastor of your parish as well. Then list some of a priest's responsibilities to the Church.

Suggested responses: serves the parish community, says Mass, provides the sacraments, and offers pastoral care to parishioners.

Deacons

- As you discuss deacons, ask participants to identify the deacons who serve your parish. Then list some of a deacon's responsibilities to the Church.

Suggested responses: performs works of charity, assists the priest during Mass, and provides pastoral care to parishioners.

"Be shepherds, with the 'odor of the sheep,' make it real, as shepherds among your flock, fishers of men."

Pope Francis, homily, March 28, 2013

The pope has many Vatican officials who help him with the day-to-day handling of Church affairs. The pope and his officials are sometimes referred to as the **Holy See**. A "see" refers to the place of authority for a bishop or archbishop.

Can the pope make a mistake?

You may have heard that the pope is infallible. That's true, but what that means is often misunderstood. It doesn't mean that the pope can never make a mistake or that he can't commit a sin. **Infallibility** means that under very special conditions, the teaching of the pope is without error through the power of the Holy Spirit. While not all teachings of the pope are infallible, Catholics are called to the humble submission of will and intellect when the pope speaks on the subject of faith and morals.

The Bishops

Jesus appointed "twelve [whom he also named apostles] that they might be with him and he might send them forth to preach and to have authority to drive out demons."

Mark 3:14–15

The Catholic Church believes that the authority Jesus gave his apostles has been passed down through the successors of the apostles—the bishops.

This authority is passed down through **ordination**, the laying on of hands, from one generation to the next. It is the responsibility of the ordained to continue the work of the apostles. A **bishop** is the chief pastor and head of a specific **diocese** (see Q11, "Places in a Catholic Church"). He oversees all matters of Church life within the boundaries of his diocese. In a very large diocese, the bishop may receive assistance from **auxiliary** (helper) **bishops**.

A diocese that is especially large or that has a significant Catholic history is called an **archdiocese**. An archdiocese is served by an **archbishop**.

Q12

Cardinal is an honorary rank the pope gives to a member of the clergy. Cardinals are allowed to vote in the election of a new pope until the age of eighty.

- *Who is the bishop of your diocese? What are his responsibilities?*

Priests

Following his resurrection, Jesus told his apostles, "Go, therefore, and make disciples of all nations, baptizing them in the name of the Father, and of the Son, and of the holy Spirit, teaching them to observe all that I have commanded you."

Matthew 28:19–20

Jesus gave his apostles special commands to follow. That's why bishops ordain priests to help them with their mission. A priest can be a diocesan priest or religious priest. A **diocesan priest** is assigned to a specific diocese and is under the authority of the local bishop. A **religious priest** is a member of a specific religious community, often called a religious order, and works in many different parts of the world at the request of local bishops.

A **pastor** is a priest who serves as the chief shepherd of the parish. He is the bishop's direct representative to the parish. Other priests appointed to a parish are called **associate pastors**.

- *Who is your parish pastor? What are some of his responsibilities?*

Deacons

After Pentecost, the apostles found themselves unable to care for the physical needs of the overwhelming number of converts to Christianity. So they said, "Brothers, select from among you seven reputable men, filled with the Spirit and wisdom, whom we shall appoint to this task, whereas we shall devote ourselves to prayer and to the ministry of the word" (Acts 6:3–4). The apostles then "prayed and laid hands on them" (Acts 6:6).

This passage from Scripture is the basis for the Catholic ordination of deacons. A **deacon** is an ordained member of the clergy, like bishops and priests, but is called to serve in different ways. His ministry is performing works of charity and assisting in liturgical celebrations. You can identify a deacon serving during Mass by his diagonal stole. A deacon can either be **transitional** (a step taken while studying for the priesthood) or **permanent** (ordained with the intention of remaining a deacon). Permanent deacons may be married but only if they were married at the time of their ordination. If a permanent deacon's wife dies, he may not remarry.

- *Is there a deacon at your church? What are some of his responsibilities?*

Religious

Religious follow Jesus' command, "If you wish to be perfect, go, sell what you have and give to [the] poor, and you will have treasure in heaven. Then come, follow me."

Matthew 19:21

In the Catholic Church, a **religious** is someone who belongs to a religious order. **Religious orders** have specific ministries, like prayer, service to the poor, teaching, or health care, in which their members take part. Religious take vows (promises) of poverty, chastity, and obedience in order to dedicate their lives to Christ completely.

People, including Catholics, sometimes use "nun" to describe all women in religious orders. The best word is actually **sister**. A **nun** is a sister who lives in a **cloister**, which means her religious order restricts contact with the outside world. A **brother** is a nonordained member of a religious order of men. A **monk** is a member of a religious order who lives in a **monastery**. He is usually focused on prayer and work as a way to draw closer to God.

The Laity

The **laity** consists of all baptized Catholics who aren't serving as priests, deacons, or bishops; this includes religious brothers and sisters. As a member of the laity, you might consider yourself a regular person, but that doesn't mean your role in the Church isn't important. The laity is the foundation of the Church. While bishops and priests are our shepherds and our guides, we are the ones who bring the light of Christ to the world!

Today laypeople are called to be disciples of Christ through service to our Church and to our brothers and sisters. We bring Christ's light through our compassion, care, and loving service. It is our responsibility to discover and acknowledge the gifts God has given us and then to use those gifts to build the reign of God here on earth.

Parish Ministries

One very practical way many laypeople serve in their parish is through parish ministries. Parish ministries are all the jobs people perform to keep the parish running smoothly and help to convey the meaning and prayerfulness of parish liturgical celebrations. Here are a few parish ministries found in most Catholic parishes:

Pastoral administrator: Your parish may have a person who helps with the pastoral care of the parish, other than the celebration of the sacraments, which require a priest.

Parish council: This is an advisory board of elected or appointed parish members who assist the pastor with administrative duties.

Lectors: These are the people who proclaim the Scriptures, except for the Gospel, at liturgies.

Extraordinary ministers (of the Eucharist): These are trained members of the laity who assist with the distribution of holy Communion.

Music ministers: These include the church musicians, **cantors** (song leaders), and members of the choir.

Altar servers: They assist at the altar during liturgies.

Religious

- As you discuss religious, ask participants to identify any religious orders or any brothers or sisters they know or have heard of. Then list some of a religious' responsibilities to the Church.

Suggested responses: prays for the Church, serves the poor, teaches, and works in health care.

The Laity

- As you discuss the laity, emphasize ways laypeople (like the participants) can help serve the Church. Some lay ministries are listed below, but take this time to mention some ministries that are particular to your parish.

Examples include: youth service groups, pro-life groups, St. Vincent DePaul chapters, rosary or other prayer groups.

- Also discuss with participants ways the lay vocation can be lived beyond the parish in the community.

Examples include: sharing your faith with friends at school or work (evangelizing), responding to hurts with love and forgiveness, helping out at home without being asked or complaining, taking opportunities to serve others (through volunteer work, tutoring peers, mentoring younger students…).

Parish Ministries

- Emphasize who's who in your own parish. Encourage participants to get to know some of these people as mentors. If possible and time allows, bring one or two of these people in to talk about their roles in the parish.
- Ask participants to share ways they are already involved in the parish (such as youth group).

As a group, create a list of all the ministries offered by your parish (some may be listed above, others may not). Then fill out that list with the name of at least one person who fulfills that ministry and how this ministry helps to strengthen your parish or community.

As a group, create a list of all the ministries offered by your parish (some may be listed above but others may not). Then fill out that list with the name of at least one person who fulfills that ministry and how this ministry helps to strengthen your parish or community.

Keeping your talents and personality in mind, in what way, large or small, can you contribute to the building of God's reign here on earth?

Journey of Faith for Teens: Inquiry, Q12 (826337)

The process by which adults are initiated into the Catholic faith throughout the United States is now called the OCIA—the Order of Christian Initiation of Adults. "Order" is a clearer translation of the Latin term for the process formerly known as the RCIA—the Rite of Christian Initiation of Adults. People preparing for baptism and reception into the Church celebrate several rites as part of the order to which those rites belong—an order whose mission is to journey in the faith. The US Conference of Catholic Bishops adopted the name change in 2021, with American dioceses introducing the name thereafter. For more information, please contact your local diocese.

Imprimi Potest: Stephen T. Rehrauer, CSsR, Provincial, Denver Province, the Redemptorists.

Imprimatur: "In accordance with CIC 827, permission to publish has been granted on March 29, 2016, by the Most Reverend Edward M. Rice, Auxiliary Bishop, Archdiocese of St. Louis. Permission to publish is an indication that nothing contrary to Church teaching is contained in this work. It does not imply any endorsement of the opinions expressed in the publication; nor is any liability assumed by this permission."

Journey of Faith for Teens © 2000, 2016 Liguori Publications, Liguori, MO 63057. All rights reserved. No part of this publication may be reproduced, distributed, stored, transmitted, or posted in any form by any means without prior written permission. To order, visit Liguori.org or call 800-325-9521. Liguori Publications, a nonprofit corporation, is an apostolate of the Redemptorists. To learn more about the Redemptorists, visit Redemptorists.com.

© 2023 Liguori Publications. Photocopying prohibited

Editors of 2016 edition: Theresa Nienaber and Pat Fosarelli, MD, DMin.
Design: Lorena Mitre Jimenez. Images: Shutterstock.

Scripture texts in this work are taken from the *New American Bible*, revised edition ©2010, 1991, 1986, 1970 Confraternity of Christian Doctrine, Washington, D.C., and are used by permission of the copyright owner. All Rights Reserved. No part of the New American Bible may be reproduced in any form without permission in writing from the copyright owner. Excerpts from English translation of the *Catechism of the Catholic Church* for the United States of America © 1994 United States Catholic Conference, Inc. —*Libreria Editrice Vaticana*; English translation of the Catechism of the Catholic Church: Modifications from the Editio Typica © 1997 United States Catholic Conference, Inc. —*Libreria Editrice Vaticana*. Compliant with *The Roman Missal, Third Edition*.

Printed in the United States of America.
Third Edition.

Journaling

Keeping your talents and personality in mind, in what way, large or small, can you contribute to the building of God's reign here on earth?

Closing Prayer

Close with Ephesians 4:11–16, which describes the need for ministries within the early Church.

Looking Ahead

Before your next lesson, take time to think about how each of these roles requires different skills. What kinds of skills do each of these roles require? What skills has God given you that might fit with these, or other, ministries.

Q13: The Church as Community

Catechism: 74–95

Objectives

- Recognize the visible "Church" as both the formal institution and the living, united people of God.
- Identify all Christians as members of the Church—Christ's Mystical Body.
- Describe how all Christians work together in the Church with corresponding roles and duties.
- Describe how the "Church," in Christ, possesses and embraces the fullness of truth.

Leader Meditation

John 14:15–31

The Church founded by Jesus Christ continues through the guidance and workings of the Holy Spirit, who dwells in every member. To understand the unity and power of the Church with its diverse membership, we must first believe that it is guided by the Holy Spirit working through its members. Though individuals make mistakes and are sometimes misguided, the people of God, as the Church, do not wander aimlessly.

Leader Preparation

- Read the lesson, this lesson plan, the Scripture passage, and the *Catechism* sections.
- If you have any books, handouts, or guides of holy people and saints for the activity gather those together.
- Be familiar with the vocabulary terms for this lesson: Church, Mystical Body. Definitions are available in this guide's glossary.

Welcome

Greet participants as they arrive. Check for supplies and immediate needs. Solicit questions or comments about the previous session and/or share new information and findings. Begin promptly.

Opening Scripture

John 14:15–31

Begin by explaining that Jesus has given us the Holy Spirit to watch over and guide his Church. The Church is not a building. The Church is people bound together by faith in Jesus Christ and led by the power of the Holy Spirit. Ask a volunteer to light the candle and read aloud. Before beginning your discussion of the lesson handout, ask participants to think about ***"what it means for the Holy Spirit to be our advocate and how the Church keeps us from being orphans in our faith."***

> The apostles entrusted the "Sacred deposit" of the faith...to the whole of the Church. "By adhering to [this heritage] the entire holy people, united to its pastors, remains always faithful to the teaching of the apostles, to the brotherhood, to the breaking of bread and the prayers."
>
> CCC 84

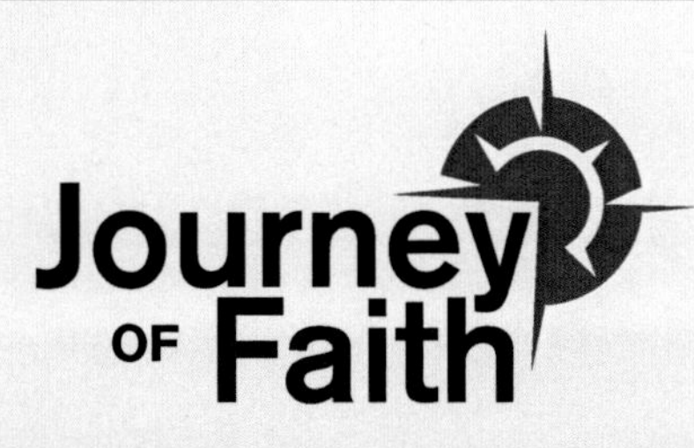

Q13
INQUIRY

In Short:

- The Church is both a formal institution and a living body.
- All Christians are part of Christ's Mystical Body.
- Christians work together in Christ's body with unique roles and duties.
- In Christ, the Church possesses the fullness of truth.

The Church as Community

Walter and Rita, the parents of nine grown children, were facing a problem. Their children lived all over the city, and it was hard for everyone to get together. But Walter and Rita wanted to stay close to their children and be a big part of their grandchildren's lives.

So Walter came up with a plan. Every Sunday evening, he and Rita cooked a large dinner and gave all nine children and their families an open invitation to come over. Dinner was at six o'clock, and card games or board games came out at seven. The children could stay for both dinner and games—or just one or the other. It didn't matter to Walter and Rita. They just wanted to offer their children and grandchildren the opportunity to stay connected.

The Sunday evening meals were a success. Everyone made an effort to stop by. The games became a tradition that sometimes lasted well into the evening. As the family grew, card tables had to be set at the ends of the big family table to accommodate everyone. And while the family sometimes got tired of Grandpa Walter's famous beef stroganoff, no one ever got tired of Sunday evening games and conversation.

Sometimes people ask, "Why do I have to go to church on Sunday? Isn't it good enough to just pray and talk to God on my own?"

To remain tied to one another through our faith in Jesus Christ, we have to spend time as a "family." Relationships and families can't thrive and develop without members spending time with one another. You probably know what it's like to lose touch with old friends because you get busy with other things—you might still be friends, but you don't feel as close. The Catholic Church has long recognized that its members can only grow as the family of God if they take time for worship, thanksgiving, and celebration.

When you think about "church" you might think of a building, the pope and bishops, or the Mass. For mature Catholics, however, **Church** is much more. The truth is expressed at the beginning of Mass.

> *The grace of our Lord Jesus Christ, and the love of God, and the fellowship of the Holy Spirit be with you all.*

It is here that our unity as Christians lies. The Church is people; people united, not by a building or a bishop, but by faith in Jesus Christ.

The Second Vatican Council, a gathering of the world's bishops, was convened by the pope in the 1960s for guidance and teaching of the Church. A Vatican II document describes the Church as "a people made one with the unity of the Father, the Son, and Holy Spirit" (Dogmatic

TEENS

© 2023 Liguori Publications. Photocopying prohibited

CCC 74–95, 946–48

The Church as Community

- After reading the lesson introduction, ask the participants to share rituals that hold their families and friendships together.
- Ask the participants if they feel it is important to attend Sunday Mass regularly. Why or why not? Then ask participants if they could still have a meaningful friendship or relationship if they never spent time with the other person. Try to connect participating in Mass to building a relationship with God and your parish community.

Q13

- As a group or in pairs, have participants look up the Scripture passages in the sidebar.

Colossians 1:18: (Christ is the head of the Church; Christ is the beginning or first born of the Church.)

Ephesians 2:19–22: (Catholics are "fellow citizens" with the holy ones and other Catholics; the Church is part of a structure with Jesus as the capstone and the apostles and prophets as the foundation.)

Galatians 3:26–29: (All the baptized are united with Jesus, and united with each other in Jesus.)

INQUIRY

JOURNEY OF FAITH

Constitution on the Church, *[Lumen Gentium]*, 4). The Church is the community of all those who have been drawn into the life of God. The Church is the real and living presence of Jesus Christ here in our world, continually leading people to God. The Church is a people with one "soul"—the Holy Spirit dwelling in their hearts.

- *Why is it important for Catholics to put time and effort into their parish communities?*

In sacred Scripture, Jesus makes it clear that prayer as a community, not just as individuals, is extremely important.

Take a moment to look up one of the Bible passages below. How does the Bible describe the Church?

Colossians 1:18 Ephesians 2:19–22
Galatians 3:26–29

What Does St. Paul Mean By Calling Us "Christ's Body?"

> *"As a body is one though it has many parts, and all the parts of the body, though many, are one body, so also Christ."*
>
> 1 Corinthians 12:12

Paul uses the terms "body of Christ" and "church" interchangeably. The word church is rooted in the Greek word *ekklesia*, which means "an assembly of people called forth by God."

Christ calls us to bring him to the world through our love and community. He tells us, "This is how all will know that you are my disciples, if you have love for one another" (John 13:35). It is the work of the Church to be Christ's body here on earth. During his life on earth, Jesus possessed his own physical body, but now we are the ones who act as Christ's body on earth.

We give Christ our lips to speak his words of love and to comfort the lost. We give him our ears to listen to the troubled. We give him our arms to hold the lonely and the sick. We give him our hearts to bring compassion and hope to a despairing world. When we forgive, Jesus forgives. When we heal, Jesus heals. Through our love, Christ's love takes human form.

- *Can you think of a time someone was Christ's body for you?*

Paul also says that we each have different gifts. We represent different parts of Christ's body. "We, though many, are one body in Christ and individually parts of one another. Since we have gifts that differ according to the grace given to us" (Romans 12:5–6). Whether our gifts are academic, athletic, social, musical, artistic, creative, or yet to be discovered, we are all parts of the body of Christ. Without each of us (no matter how insignificant we may feel), Christ's body is in some way incomplete.

The Mystical Body

Because being a member of the Church means being a part of the body of Christ, Catholics sometimes use the term **Mystical Body** to describe the Church. This Mystical Body includes every member of the Church, not just those with physical bodies here on earth. Members of the Mystical Body in purgatory are in the process of being perfected before they enter heaven. Those in heaven are interceding to God on our behalf.

The Church is the Body of Christ. It is also an assembly of the saints. The saints are God's holy ones, those perfected in holiness and those seeking to be perfected, those who stand before the Throne of God and those who continue the pilgrimage of life with their eyes set on Christ and pursuing life in Christ. These are united with one another in grace, prayer, and good works (see CCC 946–948).

Q13

What Does St. Paul Mean by Calling Us "Christ's Body?"

- Ask participants to share instances of when they were or had someone be Christ's body for them.

The Mystical Body

- Stress the importance of every part of the human body and every member of the body of Christ.
- Give participants time to reflect on the question posed at the end of this section. If you have time, ask volunteers to share their responses with the group.

What this means for us is that we are called to be members of Christ's Mystical Body not only during our earthly life, but in our eternal life. It also means that those Catholics who have come before us are still a part of us. Those souls in heaven intercede for us not because it's their celestial job, but because we're still united as family in the body of Christ.

> *"If [one] part [of the body of Christ] suffers, all the parts suffer with it; if one part is honored, all the parts share its joy"*
>
> 1 Corinthians 12:26

- *What does being part of the Mystical Body of Christ mean to you?*

Did Jesus Intend to Establish a Church?

We know Jesus wanted us to live as a close community because he always gathered his friends and followers around him and called them his flock. He requested that they pray together and taught them the message of love he wanted them to proclaim.

These early Christians believed that Christ wished to establish a Church (Matthew 16:18) with leaders who would make decisions through the power of God (Matthew 18:18). They believed that Christ gave them the Eucharist (Luke 22:14–20) and a guiding commandment (Matthew 22:39).

Jesus, however, did not leave a clear-cut plan or set of directions telling us exactly how to build his Church.

> *"And so I say to you, you are Peter, and upon this rock I will build my church, and the gates of the netherworld shall not prevail against it"*
>
> Matthew 16:18

However, Jesus backed up all his words, teachings, and commands with his personal example. Through his death and resurrection he shows us that he is the Way, the Truth, and the Life of the world. Jesus also left us the Holy Spirit to be our guide and a source of strength. The first Christians used all these gifts in the creation of the Church.

Looking at Some of the Things That Have Been Done in the History of the Church, How Can It Claim to be Guided by God?

The Church is made up of human beings who are not perfect, and therefore the Church has made decisions and taken actions that have been less than perfect. At times, human actions, in the name of the Church, have contradicted the teachings of Jesus. The Church has had leaders who failed the Church because of the power of greed, prejudice, and other wrongs.

Jesus must have known that those who would lead his followers were subject to failure. After all, Jesus chose Peter as the Church's foundation, and Jesus was fully aware of Peter's human weaknesses (John 21:15–18). The early Church was burdened by the same problems as the Church of our modern world—liars and hypocrites (Acts 5:1–11), unfair treatment (Acts 6:1), disagreement over religious issues (Acts 15), abuse of power by Church leaders (Acts 8:9–24), and even sermons so long they put people to sleep (Acts 20:7–12)!

While the followers of Jesus sometimes failed him, there were many more who were true heroes. They proclaimed and lived the gospel with courage and faithfulness in their everyday lives. In our own time, the Church has produced individuals who are universally recognized for their outstanding goodness and holiness. Our task, as members of the body of Christ, is to make our Lord visibly present to those among whom we live, learn, work, and play.

Did Jesus Intend to Establish a Church?

- Emphasize that the Bible is a primary source of revelation for Catholics but that tradition is also a legitimate, sacred resource of telling God's truth.
- If participants express concerns that Church membership results in unhealthy conformity, provide examples of the great diversity within the Church—various liturgical rites and languages, worship and prayer styles, religious orders, ministries and forms of stewardship, and causes for which one can pursue social justice (which encompass both political parties). You can also refer back to the section on Christ's Mystical Body. If all members of the body were the same part, the Church wouldn't be able to function as a whole.

How Can the Church Claim to be Guided by God?

- Emphasize that like any, indeed *all*, institutions, members of the Church make mistakes. Though guided by the Spirit, Church leaders are humans subject to the same temptations of greed, power, and self-indulgence. When any member of the Church fails or falls short, the response should be to seek mercy, reconciliation, and to make amends.

There are many inspiring examples of Catholics living as the body of Christ. With a partner or on your own, find one biblical holy person or modern saint and do some research. Find at least one way in which this person was Christ's body in the world. Share this with the rest of the group.

There are many inspiring examples of Catholics living as the body of Christ. With a partner or on your own, find one biblical holy person or modern saint and do some research. Find at least one way they were Christ's body in the world. Share with the rest of the group.

Read St. Paul's Letter to the Romans 12:3–8. As a member of the body of Christ, which "part" are you?

Keep in mind your special gifts and talents, however small you may think they are.

Journey of Faith for Teens: Inquiry, Q13 (826337)

The process by which adults are initiated into the Catholic faith throughout the United States is now called the OCIA—the Order of Christian Initiation of Adults. "Order" is a clearer translation of the Latin term for the process formerly known as the RCIA—the Rite of Christian Initiation of Adults. People preparing for baptism and reception into the Church celebrate several rites as part of the order to which those rites belong—an order whose mission is to journey in the faith. The US Conference of Catholic Bishops adopted the name change in 2021, with American dioceses introducing the name thereafter. For more information, please contact your local diocese.

Imprimi Potest: Stephen T. Rehrauer, CSsR, Provincial, Denver Province, the Redemptorists.

Imprimatur: "In accordance with CIC 827, permission to publish has been granted on March 29, 2016, by the Most Reverend Edward M. Rice, Auxiliary Bishop, Archdiocese of St. Louis. Permission to publish is an indication that nothing contrary to Church teaching is contained in this work. It does not imply any endorsement of the opinions expressed in the publication; nor is any liability assumed by this permission."

Journey of Faith for Teens © 2000, 2016 Liguori Publications, Liguori, MO 63057. All rights reserved. No part of this publication may be reproduced, distributed, stored, transmitted, or posted in any form by any means without prior written permission. To order, visit Liguori.org or call 800-325-9521. Liguori Publications, a nonprofit corporation, is an apostolate of the Redemptorists. To learn more about the Redemptorists, visit Redemptorists.com.

© 2023 Liguori Publications. Photocopying prohibited

Editors of 2016 edition: Theresa Nienaber and Pat Fosarelli, MD, DMin. Design: Lorena Mitre Jimenez. Images: Shutterstock.

Scripture texts in this work are taken from the *New American Bible*, revised edition ©2010, 1991, 1986, 1970 Confraternity of Christian Doctrine, Washington, D.C., and are used by permission of the copyright owner. All Rights Reserved. No part of the New American Bible may be reproduced in any form without permission in writing from the copyright owner. Excerpts from English translation of the *Catechism of the Catholic Church* for the United States of America © 1994 United States Catholic Conference, Inc. —*Libreria Editrice Vaticana;* English translation of the Catechism of the Catholic Church: Modifications from the Editio Typica © 1997 United States Catholic Conference, Inc. —*Libreria Editrice Vaticana.* Compliant with *The Roman Missal, Third Edition.*

Printed in the United States of America.
Third Edition.

Journaling

Read St. Paul's Letter to the Romans 12:3–8. As a member of the body of Christ, which "part" are you? Keep in mind your special gifts and talents, however small you may think they are.

Closing Prayer

Ask participants to state any special intentions. If you haven't already taught students how to share and respond to a petition (using the call and response "we pray to the Lord" and "Lord, hear our prayer"), this is a good time to begin practicing this tradition.

Looking Ahead

In Mary, the Mother of God, we are given a great inspiration for living as the body of Christ. Before next class, have participants think about how the Catholic Church honors Mary. Have participants write down any practices they find confusing or meaningful to share with the group.

Q14: Mary

Catechism: 963–972

Objectives:

- List several key titles of Mary and their origins and meanings.
- Explain how major teachings about Mary are tied to teachings about Jesus.
- Discover the intercessory power of Mary.
- Gain comfort and confidence in honoring, reflecting on, and asking for Mary's prayers.

Leader Meditation

Luke 1:46–55

Lord, may my life magnify your presence here on earth. Like Mary, may I serve your people with humility and compassion. Like a loving mother or father, may I love and respect the young people in my care, accepting them for who they are. May I teach with patience and understanding. Amen.

Leader Preparation

- Read the lesson, this lesson plan, the Scripture passage, and the *Catechism* sections.
- If you have any resources on Mary for the activity, organize them. *These can include books, prayer cards, information on Marian icons or apparitions, or information on churches or shrines dedicated to Mary.*
- Try to find a version of John Michael Talbot's song "Holy Is His Name" for the closing prayer.
- Be familiar with the vocabulary terms for this lesson: honor, worship, dogma. Definitions can be found in this guide's glossary.

Welcome

Greet participants as they arrive. Check for supplies and immediate needs. Solicit questions or comments about the previous session and/or share new information and findings. Begin promptly.

Opening Scripture

Luke 1:46–55

Ask for a volunteer to light the candle and read the passage aloud. Explain that this passage is known as Mary's Magnificat. In this passage, the word *magnifies* means "glorifies." In order to magnify God, Mary subjects herself completely to God's will. Before beginning your discussion of the lesson handout, ask participants to think about ***"how Mary's prayer magnifies the Lord."***

> Mary's role in the Church is inseparable from her union with Christ and flows directly from it. This union of the mother with the Son in the work of salvation is made manifest from the time of Christ's virginal conception up to his death.
>
> CCC 964

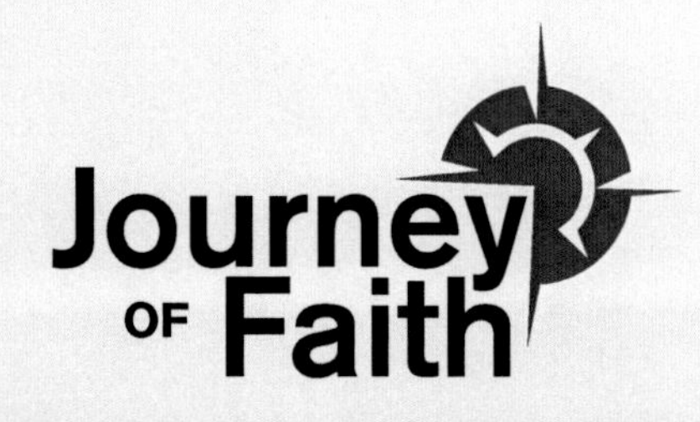

Q14 INQUIRY

In Short:

- Mary intercedes for us as the Mother.
- Jesus and Mary share a strong connection.
- Mary's titles share unique aspects of who she is to us.

Mary

Mary's Song of Praise (The Magnificat)

> "My soul proclaims the greatness of the Lord; my spirit rejoices in God my savior. For he has looked upon his handmaid's lowliness; behold, from now on will all ages call me blessed. The Mighty One has done great things for me, and holy is his name. His mercy is from age to age to those who fear him. He has shown might with his arm, dispersed the arrogant of mind and heart. He has thrown down the rulers from their thrones but lifted up the lowly. The hungry he has filled with good things; the rich he has sent away empty. He has helped Israel his servant, remembering his mercy, according to his promise to our fathers, to Abraham and to his descendants forever"
>
> Luke 1:46–55

Mary's beautiful song of praise to God is sometimes called Mary's canticle or the Magnificat. It is a statement of her faith in God—filled with hope and trust—at a time when her future seemed uncertain.

When the angel Gabriel visited Mary with the news of God's plan, Mary was a very young woman—not much older than you are now. At first, she was puzzled by the words of the angel (see Luke 1:29). Her plans hadn't included being the mother of the Son of God. At first, she responded to Gabriel with feelings of confusion and doubt: "How can this be?" (Luke 1:34). By allowing herself to be open to the power of the Holy Spirit, she found the strength to ultimately respond with her fiat, or her great yes: "May it be done to me according to your word" (Luke 1:38).

Mary was very much one of us. She was fully human. She felt all the emotions we feel—confusion, fear, doubt—and great joy. Despite her feelings of doubt and confusion, Mary chose to trust in God. She allowed God to change the course of her life forever, but the Bible makes it clear that the choice was not an easy one for her. Mary is someone we can relate to. Through her words and actions, she becomes a model for our lives.

- *What are some areas in your life where you need help in saying "yes" to God?*
- *Read Mary's song of praise again. How do her words offer you hope for your life?*

Why Do Catholics Honor Mary?

> *"By her complete adherence to the Father's will, to his Son's redemptive work, and to every prompting of the Holy Spirit, the Virgin Mary is the Church's model of faith and charity."*
>
> CCC 967

TEENS

© 2023 Liguori Publications. Photocopying prohibited

CCC 963–972

Mary

- As the points made in the handout are read and discussed, continually emphasize the humanity of Mary. She was just like us in all things but sin, and not much older than many teen participants!
- Allow participants to share their personal response to the Magnificat after the opening Scripture, especially knowing that Mary wasn't much older than them when she was asked to be the Mother of God.
- Ask the participants to give examples from Scripture of when Mary felt confused, frightened, angry, courageous, or joyful. Show them how to find the infancy narrative in the Gospel of Luke (chapters 1–2) or the crucifixion scenes (toward the end of each Gospel).

Suggested responses include: Luke 1:29 (confusion and fear); Luke 1:38 (courage and faith in God); Luke 2:33 (amazement); Luke 2:48 (anger or frustration); and Luke 2:51 (courage).

- Ask the participants for examples of how they can say "yes" to God or areas they struggle to say it. Emphasize that it was Mary's willingness to say "yes" to the very difficult things God asked of her that makes her so special in the eyes of the Church.

Why Do Catholics Honor Mary?

- Discuss why worshiping God is different from honoring Mary

Suggested responses include: We worship only God because he is our Creator and Savior. We honor Mary because she lived a life of great sacrifice and virtue, and we ask her to help us live more like her.

Discuss the reflection questions as a group. Share the role Mary plays in your own faith if you need help getting the discussion started, or ask participants if they struggle to see Mary as an integral part of their faith. *If participants struggle to include Mary as part of their faith, remind them that by loving Mary we are following Jesus' example.*

How Do Catholics Honor Mary?

- Discuss ways the Catholic Church honors Mary (keep a list somewhere to collect your thoughts).

Suggested responses include: naming churches in her honor, building statues, creating images or icons of Mary, praying for her intercession through prayers like the rosary or Magnificat, and trying to imitate her life.

INQUIRY

JOURNEY OF FAITH

Gabriel called Mary "favored one" (Luke 1:28), and Mary's cousin, Elizabeth, upon seeing her, cried out, "Most blessed are you among women, and blessed is the fruit of your womb" (Luke 1:42). Catholics throughout the ages have continued this tradition of honoring Mary. While Jesus Christ is the center of our faith, Catholics often look to Mary as the perfect example of Christian humility and trust in God.

It is important to understand the difference between worshiping God and honoring Mary. Even many Catholics confuse this point. To **honor** someone means to hold him or her in great respect or high regard. To **worship** means to show reverence for a god. Catholics worship only God the Father, Son, and Holy Spirit.

Similarly, when Catholics pray the Hail Mary, we do not pray to Mary. We are honoring her with words taken directly from Scripture (Luke 1:28, 42) and then asking her to pray for us because of her unique closeness to our Lord.

God the Father honors Mary. In Luke's Gospel, the angel Gabriel tells Mary that she has found favor with God (Luke 1:28, 30). God chooses Mary from among all women to be the Mother of Jesus, "the Word made flesh." God entrusts this holy young woman with the Light of the World. Because of her "yes," we would have a Savior.

Jesus honors Mary. Jesus shows special respect for his Mother by granting her requests as in the marriage feast at Cana (John 2:1–11) and by holding her up as an example of one who hears the word of God and lives it (Luke 8:21). At the time of his death, Jesus makes sure Mary will be cared for by his "beloved disciple" (John 19:26–27).

Even the friends and disciples of Jesus sometimes brought their problems to Mary, trusting in her closeness to her Son. At the wedding feast at Cana, Mary steps in to help when the wine begins to run low. Still, Mary reminds the disciples that they must rely only on Jesus with the words, "Do whatever he tells you" (John 2:5). Mary also prayed with the disciples while they waited for the coming of the Spirit (Acts 1:14). These events take on an even greater significance when we understand that, at the time of Jesus, women had very little social standing.

Q14

OUR MOTHER OF PERPETUAL HELP

OUR LADY OF GUADALUPE

The early Christian Church honored Mary. Written within the century following the death and resurrection of Jesus, the Gospels reflect the thinking of the early Church. As early as the year 150, Christian artists began painting pictures of Mary holding the Infant Jesus. The Catholic Church's devotion to Mary is deeply rooted in tradition.

- *What role does Mary play in your faith?*
- *How do you understand Mary's role in the Church?*

How Do Catholics Honor Mary?

The Hail Mary

Hail Mary, full of grace, the Lord is with you; blessed are you among women, and blessed is the fruit of your womb, Jesus. Holy Mary, Mother of God, pray for us sinners, now and at the hour of our death. Amen.

Just as we erect buildings, ballparks, and other special places in the name of respected public figures, so Catholics often name churches in Mary's honor. And just as we fashion statues of great men and women, Catholics often use images of Mary to help them reflect on her holiness and pure, humble life. In doing this, we aren't worshiping Mary, rather we're holding her up as inspiration. Mary reminds us that when we simply say "yes," we bring Christ to our world.

E AND POPE FRANCIS

OUR LADY OF LOURDES

Catholics also consider Mary to be a powerful intercessor with God—one who will pray with us and for us. While it is not necessary to ask Mary to pray for us, when we call on her, we share in her holiness and have someone praying for us who is intimately connected to Jesus. Devotion to Mary never replaces dedication to God. God and Mary are not in competition. All power, all love, all healing, all graces, come from God alone. When we pray the Hail Mary, we are asking the Mother of Jesus to present our heartfelt needs to her Son.

Praying the rosary is another way Catholics have traditionally honored Mary. This form of devotion dates back to the ninth century. As we pray the rosary, we recall important events in the life of Jesus, many of which remind us of Mary's key role in the life of our Lord and in our own salvation.

Perhaps the most important way Catholics can honor Mary is by the honest attempt to imitate her life.

> *"In the meantime the Mother of Jesus...is the image and beginning of the Church as it is to be perfected in the world to come."*
>
> *CCC* 972

What Else Does the Catholic Church Teach About Mary?

The word **dogma** refers to an official Church teaching. The dogma of the immaculate conception tells us that Mary was born free from original sin. Put another way, Mary was never controlled by hate, prejudice, greed, or selfishness. Her life was guided by love. Her motivation was love. Her decisions were based on love. There was no room in Mary's heart for sin.

This doesn't mean that Mary wasn't fully human or that she didn't feel the same emotions we feel. Actually, the opposite is true. Because sin had no power over her, there was nothing to keep her from understanding us and relating to us perfectly. Mary lived a life of faith and service, just as we strive to do.

Because she was the Mother of our Lord, neither sin nor death touched her soul or her body. The Church also teaches that, at her death, Mary was taken up, body and soul, into heaven. This is called the assumption.

Catholics also refer to Mary as ever-virgin, meaning that Mary chose to remain a virgin even after the birth of Jesus. Mary dedicated her life to the love of God.

When the Church calls Mary "the Mother of God," it does not mean that Mary was the source of Jesus' divine (godly) nature. Mary was the Mother of his human nature and there was no time when the human Jesus was not God. Mary said "yes" to being Mother to "God in the flesh."

Mary is also considered to be the "Mother of the Church." Just as she prayed with the first disciples of Jesus as they waited for the coming of the Spirit (Acts 1:14), so she prays continually with and for the Church today. Through her loving example, she has led many believers to the grace of God.

In praise of all that God had done for her, Mary prayed her glorious Magnificat (Luke 1:46–55). Today we are proud to be numbered among the generations that call Mary blessed.

What Else Does the Catholic Church Teach About Mary?

- Remind participants that the immaculate conception refers to *Mary's* conception (in Anne's womb), not Jesus'.
- If questioned about Mary as ever-virgin, respond with the Protoevangelium of James written about AD 120, and that St. Augustine and even Martin Luther upheld this.

Mary has been given many titles as an intercessor of the Church including: Undoer of Knots, Mother of Perpetual Help, Our Lady of Angels, Our Lady of Guadalupe, and many others. With a partner or on your own, pick and research one title of Mary to share with your group. What about the title you chose resonated with you?

JOURNEY OF FAITH **INQUIRY**

Mary has been given many titles as an intercessor of the Church including: Undoer of Knots, Our Mother of Perpetual Help, Our Lady of Angels, Our Lady of Guadalupe, and many others.

With a partner or on your own, pick and research one title of Mary to share with your group. What about the title you chose resonated with you?

Our faith grows every time we give God our simple "yes."

Write about one situation in your life right now in which you can choose to do or say what is right or good. How can you, like Mary, say "yes" to God?

***Journey of Faith for Teens: Inquiry*, Q14 (826337)**

The process by which adults are initiated into the Catholic faith throughout the United States is now called the OCIA—the Order of Christian Initiation of Adults. "Order" is a clearer translation of the Latin term for the process formerly known as the RCIA—the Rite of Christian Initiation of Adults. People preparing for baptism and reception into the Church celebrate several rites as part of the order to which those rites belong—an order whose mission is to journey in the faith. The US Conference of Catholic Bishops adopted the name change in 2021, with American dioceses introducing the name thereafter. For more information, please contact your local diocese.

Imprimi Potest: Stephen T. Rehrauer, CSsR, Provincial, Denver Province, the Redemptorists.

Imprimatur: "In accordance with CIC 827, permission to publish has been granted on March 29, 2016, by the Most Reverend Edward M. Rice, Auxiliary Bishop, Archdiocese of St. Louis. Permission to publish is an indication that nothing contrary to Church teaching is contained in this work. It does not imply any endorsement of the opinions expressed in the publication; nor is any liability assumed by this permission."

Journey of Faith for Teens © 2000, 2016 Liguori Publications, Liguori, MO 63057. All rights reserved. No part of this publication may be reproduced, distributed, stored, transmitted, or posted in any form by any means without prior written permission. To order, visit Liguori.org or call 800-325-9521. Liguori Publications, a nonprofit corporation, is an apostolate of the Redemptorists. To learn more about the Redemptorists, visit Redemptorists.com.

© 2023 Liguori Publications. Photocopying prohibited

Editors of 2016 edition: Theresa Nienaber and Pat Fosarelli, MD, DMin. Design: Lorena Mitre Jimenez. Images: Shutterstock.

Scripture texts in this work are taken from the *New American Bible*, revised edition ©2010, 1991, 1986, 1970 Confraternity of Christian Doctrine, Washington, D.C., and are used by permission of the copyright owner. All Rights Reserved. No part of the New American Bible may be reproduced in any form without permission in writing from the copyright owner. Excerpts from English translation of the *Catechism of the Catholic Church* for the United States of America © 1994 United States Catholic Conference, Inc. —*Libreria Editrice Vaticana*; English translation of the Catechism of the Catholic Church: Modifications from the Editio Typica © 1997 United States Catholic Conference, Inc. —*Libreria Editrice Vaticana*. Compliant with *The Roman Missal, Third Edition*.

Printed in the United States of America.
Third Edition.

Journaling

Our faith grows every time we give God our simple "yes." Write about one situation in your life right now in which you can choose to do or say what is right or good. How can you, like Mary, say "yes" to God?

Closing Prayer

Dim the lights and listen to the words of Mary's Magnificat in John Michael Talbot's song "Holy Is His Name." If the song is unavailable, pray the Hail Mary.

Looking Ahead

There are many other saints and holy people honored by the Church. Before the next class, have participants research one or two of these people and how they are honored by the Church.

Q15: The Saints

Catechism: 946–59; 2683–84

Objectives

- Distinguish between honoring the saints and worshiping God.
- Define canonized saints as humans who lived virtuous lives for God and are now in heaven.
- Consider the differences between being "holy" and being "perfect."
- Recall the steps of the canonization process and criteria.
- Explore the lives of the saints, looking for patrons, mentors, and their own sacramental name.

Leader Meditation

Prayer

Lord Jesus, I remember your promise, "I will not leave you orphans." You have sent your Holy Spirit to be with us, to guide us, to lead us to heaven. All who are filled with your Spirit are with us in the communion of saints. Grant that I may always recognize their presence and be guided toward holiness by their example. Help me to encourage the young people in my care to seek out and follow those whom you have sent to teach us and to lead us. Amen.

Leader Preparation

- Read the lesson, this lesson plan, and the *Catechism* sections.
- Collect any books or other resources on the lives of the saints (such as *Butler's Lives of the Saints*) that will be useful for the activity or the lesson itself.
- Be familiar with the vocabulary terms for this lesson: canonization, saint. Definitions can be found in this guide's glossary.

Welcome

Greet participants as they arrive. Check for supplies and immediate needs. Solicit questions or comments about the previous session and/or share new information and findings. Begin promptly.

Opening Scripture

Instead of a reading from Scripture, choose a story from the lives of the saints. Light the candle and read the story of this special saint to the group. Then ask the participants if they can relate to the saint they have just read about. For example, as a young man, Francis of Assisi loved to socialize and party. Saint Thérèse of Lisieux often found it difficult to pray. God chooses even those who struggle with the things of this world to become saints. Before beginning your discussion of the lesson handout, ask participants, ***"How might saints inspire us to live our faith better?"***

> The witnesses who have preceded us into the kingdom, especially those whom the Church recognizes as saints, share in the living tradition of prayer by the example of their lives, the transmission of their writings, and their prayer today.
>
> CCC 2683

Q15

INQUIRY

In Short:

- The saints weren't always perfect.
- The saints are our mentors.
- The saints intercede on our behalf.

The Saints

- *Describe someone you know whom you would consider to be holy.*
- *Has this person's way of life affected the way you live?*

Your answers will tell you a lot about why the Catholic Church recognizes saints. Like the person you described, saints were real people who led holy lives that we look to as role models. The person you described as holy may be unknown to the rest of the world. By honoring saints, the Church makes sure that everyone can benefit from the grace of God that shines through holy people.

Please choose which statements are true and which are false.

T	F	
❐	❐	1. Saints were hermits who withdrew from the world.
❐	❐	2. Saints never made mistakes or failed.
❐	❐	3. Saints liked to have fun and laugh.
❐	❐	4. Saints never got angry.

1. False. There are many saints who lived in the world. Saint Frances of Rome was a wife and the mother of three children. She converted her home into a hospital and shelter for victims of war. Saint Frances Cabrini lived in slums and cooked her food in tenement courtyards to be close to people who needed her most. She was just as likely to be found laying brick as talking to bishops.
2. False. Saints were not perfect! Many saints failed at what they tried and certainly made mistakes and sinned. Saint Anthony of Padua left a monastery because he wanted to be a missionary. But he fell sick as soon as he got off the boat and never preached. On his way home to Portugal, he was shipwrecked in Italy and couldn't even get a job as a dishwasher! The holiness of the saints was not in worldly success but in their desire to do God's will.
3. True. Many people assume all saints were serious and didn't know how to have fun. But the opposite is true. Saint Teresa of Ávila said, "Lord, deliver me from gloomy-faced saints," and that's the way she lived. Saint John Bosco delighted poor children with magic tricks and acrobatics as he taught them about their faith. People thought he was crazy for taking responsibility for so many children without money. One day two priests came in a carriage to take him to the mental hospital. John, who had been warned, agreed easily to "a ride in the country." Then he very politely said, "After you," to the priests. As soon as the priests were in the carriage, John slammed the carriage door and yelled to the driver, "To the mental hospital!"

The saints' joy comes from their love of God and their faith that God loved them.

TEENS

© 2023 Liguori Publications. Photocopying prohibited

CCC 946–959; 2683–2684

The Saints

- Discuss the questions in the lesson introduction as a group. Be prepared to share an example of your own.

True or False?

- Give participants time to go through the T/F questions on their own, encourage them not to look ahead at the answers, and answer based on what they think now.
- As you go through the explanations of each answer, ask participants to share why they think someone might choose the wrong answer or if any participants were surprised by the answer given.
- Give participants time to answer the reflection question on their own. Ask for volunteers to share their responses.

How to Become a Saint

- As you read through the process on how to become a saint, share the four stages toward sainthood in the Catholic Church: (1) servant of God, (2) venerable servant of God, (3) beatification/blessed, (4) canonized/sainthood.
- You may also emphasize that the process for a martyr to become a saint does not necessarily follow this pattern because they can be canonized without any attributed miracles.

If you have time, have participants get into groups or work on their own to create a visual aid to explain the process of canonization.

4. False. Saints struggled with the same problems we do, including anger. Saint Philip Neri went into a church to pray that God would rid him of his temper. When he left, he immediately ran into someone he disliked and got into an argument. Going back into the church, he prayed again to be rid of his temper. This time he left the church and ran into a friend—and got into a fight. He went into the church a third time and said to God, "Why didn't you answer my prayer?" God answered, "You said you wanted to get rid of your temper. I thought you wanted practice!"

Saints are not plaster statues but were real people who made mistakes, struggled, and enjoyed life. The reason these people are saints is that they faced their mistakes, their struggles, and their joys with a deep love of God and a desire to do God's will completely, no matter what the sacrifice.

- *How do these answers change or affirm your understanding of the saints and sainthood?*

How to Become a Saint

The procedure the Church uses to name a saint is called **canonization**. The canonization process begins after the death of a Catholic who has been considered holy. To be canonized, the candidate's life is examined for heroic virtue or martyrdom, orthodoxy of doctrine (which means living one's life according to Church teachings), and reputation for holiness. A candidate must have one miracle attributed to him or her after death to be **beatified**, which puts the individual one step away from sainthood. After this, one more (for a total of two) miracle must be attributed to the person before sainthood can be granted. This is not necessarily true for martyrs, who can be canonized without any miracles being attributed to them.

The title **saint** tells us that the person lived a holy life, is in heaven, and is to be honored by the universal Church. But canonization does not make a person a saint. It only recognizes what God has already done. Canonization is also a lengthy, difficult process. So while every canonized saint is holy, not every holy person has been canonized.

St. Thérèse of Lisieux

St. John Bosco

- *How would you explain the canonization process to someone who knows nothing about sainthood or the Church? Create a list, narrative, graph, or other visual.*

Do Catholics Worship Saints?

"Being more closely united to Christ, those who dwell in heaven fix the whole Church more firmly in holiness....They do not cease to intercede with the Father for us."

CCC 956

You probably have pictures of people you love around your house or in your room, but you probably don't worship the images. The reasons you keep pictures of people you care about is the same reason Catholics have statues and pictures of saints. Seeing a statue of St. Thérèse of Lisieux, who lost her mother when she was a child, might make us feel less alone when we are grieving. A picture of St. Francis of Assisi might remind us of how much he loved God's creation and make us more aware of our environment.

- *Think about the photos you have at home. Why do you keep them around?*
- *Name a particular virtue or struggle you need help with. Find a saint you can look to for inspiration.*

Do Catholics Worship Saints?

- Emphasize that the tradition of honoring the saints has been a part of the Catholic Church since its beginning. Reiterate that the saints are our role models in faith, not demigods to be worshiped or idolized. They exist for inspiration, imitation, and intercession.

If participants struggle with this teaching, try talking about it as though the saints were living people and we're going to them to ask for advice and prayers for something we're struggling with.

- You can have students respond to the reflection questions here on their own or, if you have extra time, answer the second question as a group.

Instead of having participants name a virtue they struggle with, have the group list some common struggles or just list virtues.

Suggested responses include: St. Joseph and humility, St. Monica and patience, St. Augustine and temperance, St. Agnes and chastity.

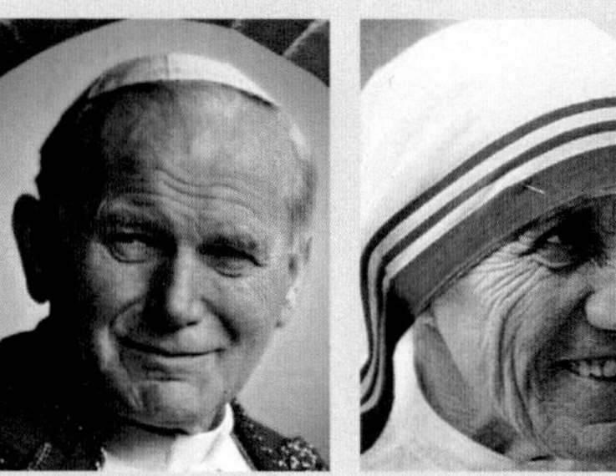

St. John Paul II

Saint Teresa of Calcutta

We don't pray to saints the same way we pray to God. Only God is worthy of worship. One definition of pray is "earnest petition." When Catholics say they pray to saints, they are not saying they worship saints. They are earnestly asking the saints to pray to God for them.

- *Have you ever asked anyone to pray for you when you were having a hard time? Why did you choose that person?*

We often ask particular saints to pray for us if we feel they have a particular interest in our problem. For example, many people ask St. Monica to pray for them if they have trouble with unanswered prayers because Monica prayed for twenty years for her son to be converted.

The question is: Why would they stop caring once they are in heaven? If St. Martin de Porres loved helping the sick so much that he gave up his food and his bed to sick people and animals, would he stop loving the sick when he went to heaven? Or would he actually love them more, since he no longer has earthly cares and anxieties weighing him down?

"It is not merely by the title of example that we cherish the memory of those in heaven; we seek, rather, that by this devotion...the whole Church in the Spirit may be strengthened."

CCC 957

We honor the saints in many different ways. We celebrate feast days, write icons, create religiously inspired art, place images and statues around our churches and homes, and say special intercessory prayers.

- *Do any of these ways of honoring saints especially appeal to you? Confuse you?*

If you aren't used to praying with the saints, you might be overwhelmed by everything the Church offers. The most important thing to remember is that we can pray with the saints simply by talking to them as friends. Here's a meditation that may help:

- Picture yourself in a place you consider holy.
- A saint (pick one you feel close to or who is meaningful to you) joins you there.
- Talk to the saint as you would a friend.
- Share the events of your day, your problems, anything at all.
- Ask the saint for advice.
- Sit in silence and keep your mind and heart open to this advice.

Saint John Vianney struggled with his studies, flunking out several times. He never would have been ordained without the constant tutoring of another priest. Yet he was so wise and compassionate that 20,000 people a year came to his tiny rural parish to confess to him.

There are saints who were twelve years old and saints who lived 100 years. There are saints from all ethnic and racial backgrounds, like Martin de Porres, Kateri Tekakwitha, Juan Diego, and Paul Miki. There are saints with disabilities, like Julia Billiart who, though unable to walk for twenty years, taught, organized boycotts, and hid priests during French persecution. There are saints who grew up homeless, like John of the Cross, and saints who grew up to be queens, like Elizabeth of Hungary.

For every struggle you can imagine, there is a saint who embraced and became holy through it. The only thing that can keep you from being a saint is your desire. Do you want to do God's will? Do you want to be transformed by God?

Q15

- If you have time, use the sidebar meditation as part of your lesson. If you don't have time, encourage participants to try it on their own.

With a partner or on your own, research a saint you feel connected to (one who shares your name, hobbies, future occupation, or other trait). Pick two to three key facts about why you think that person is a saint and share the information with the group.

JOURNEY OF FAITH **INQUIRY**

With a partner or on your own, research a saint you feel connected to, such as one who shares your name, hobbies, future occupation, and so on.

Choose two or three key facts about why you picked that saint to share with the group.

What would you like to be patron saint of?

What would you have to change to be open to God making you a saint?

Journey of Faith for Teens: Inquiry, Q15 (826337)

The process by which adults are initiated into the Catholic faith throughout the United States is now called the OCIA—the Order of Christian Initiation of Adults. "Order" is a clearer translation of the Latin term for the process formerly known as the RCIA—the Rite of Christian Initiation of Adults. People preparing for baptism and reception into the Church celebrate several rites as part of the order to which those rites belong—an order whose mission is to journey in the faith. The US Conference of Catholic Bishops adopted the name change in 2021, with American dioceses introducing the name thereafter. For more information, please contact your local diocese.

Imprimi Potest: Stephen T. Rehrauer, CSsR, Provincial, Denver Province, the Redemptorists.

Imprimatur: "In accordance with CIC 827, permission to publish has been granted on March 29, 2016, by the Most Reverend Edward M. Rice, Auxiliary Bishop, Archdiocese of St. Louis. Permission to publish is an indication that nothing contrary to Church teaching is contained in this work. It does not imply any endorsement of the opinions expressed in the publication; nor is any liability assumed by this permission."

Journey of Faith for Teens © 2000, 2016 Liguori Publications, Liguori, MO 63057. All rights reserved. No part of this publication may be reproduced, distributed, stored, transmitted, or posted in any form by any means without prior written permission. To order, visit Liguori.org or call 800-325-9521. Liguori Publications, a nonprofit corporation, is an apostolate of the Redemptorists. To learn more about the Redemptorists, visit Redemptorists.com.

© 2023 Liguori Publications. Photocopying prohibited

Editors of 2016 edition: Theresa Nienaber and Pat Fosarelli, MD, DMin.
Design: Lorena Mitre Jimenez. Images: Shutterstock.

Scripture texts in this work are taken from the *New American Bible*, revised edition ©2010, 1991, 1986, 1970 Confraternity of Christian Doctrine, Washington, D.C., and are used by permission of the copyright owner. All Rights Reserved. No part of the New American Bible may be reproduced in any form without permission in writing from the copyright owner. Excerpts from English translation of the *Catechism of the Catholic Church* for the United States of America © 1994 United States Catholic Conference, Inc. —*Libreria Editrice Vaticana*; English translation of the Catechism of the Catholic Church: Modifications from the Editio Typica © 1997 United States Catholic Conference, Inc. —*Libreria Editrice Vaticana*. Compliant with *The Roman Missal, Third Edition*.

Printed in the United States of America.
Third Edition.

Liguori PUBLICATIONS A Redemptorist Ministry

Journey of Faith

Journaling

What would you like to be patron saint of? What would you have to do to be open to God making you a saint?

Closing Prayer

Prayerfully read these words written by St. Thérèse of Lisieux, "The Little Flower":

But how shall I show my love, since love proves itself by deeds?...The only way I have of proving my love is to strew flowers before Thee—that is to say, I will let no tiny sacrifice pass, no look, no word. I wish to profit by the smallest actions, and to do them for Love. I wish to suffer for Love's sake, and for Love's sake even to rejoice: thus shall I strew flowers.

Looking Ahead

Ask participants to spend time over the next week researching the lives of saints. Encourage them to make a list of saints they feel drawn to as mentors or patrons and to use this list as they consider their own sacramental name.

Q16: Eschatology: the "Last Things"

Catechism: 675–682, 988–1001, 1020–1065

Objectives

- Distinguish between heaven and hell as the only two eternal outcomes.
- Define **purgatory** as a final purification in preparation for heaven.
- Differentiate between particular judgment and the Final Judgment.

Leader Meditation

Luke 18:8

As you prepare for this lesson, do your own examination of conscience and assess where you are on the journey of becoming "holy as he is holy" so as to inherit eternal life.

Leader Preparation

- Read the lesson, this lesson plan, and the *Catechism* sections. This may help you answer questions about Catholic teaching on the rapture or other variations of the "end times."
- Be familiar with the vocabulary terms for this lesson: eschatology, heaven, hell, purgatory. Definitions can be found in this guide's glossary.

Welcome

Greet participants as they arrive. Check for supplies and immediate needs. Solicit questions or comments about the previous session and/or share new information and findings. Begin promptly.

Opening Scripture

Luke 18:8

Ask one of the participants to light the candle and read aloud. Following the reading, allow a moment of silence, then welcome comments or questions. Before beginning your discussion of the lesson handout, ask participants, ***"What does it mean for God to make a 'right and just' decision?"***

> Christ is Lord of eternal life. Full right to pass definitive judgment on the works and hearts of men belongs to him as redeemer of the world.
>
> CCC 679

Q16 INQUIRY

In Short:

- The difference between heaven and hell
- What it means to be in purgatory
- How particular judgment and Final Judgment differ

Eschatology: the "Last Things"

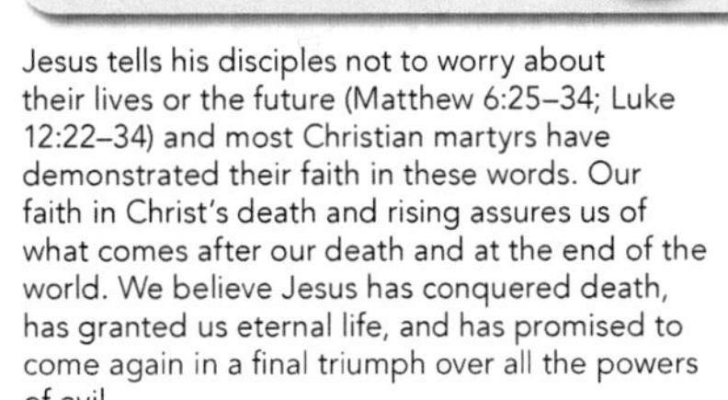

- *Do you ever worry about your future?*
- *What happens after we die?*

Jesus tells his disciples not to worry about their lives or the future (Matthew 6:25–34; Luke 12:22–34) and most Christian martyrs have demonstrated their faith in these words. Our faith in Christ's death and rising assures us of what comes after our death and at the end of the world. We believe Jesus has conquered death, has granted us eternal life, and has promised to come again in a final triumph over all the powers of evil.

Eschatology is the part of theology concerned with death, judgment, and the final destiny of the soul of humankind.

Eschatology deals with what comes:

- at the end of an individual person's life.
- at the end of human history and creation.
- at the Second Coming of Christ.

Let's follow the story of "Joe" and explore his life and afterlife all the way to the Second Coming of Christ. Then we'll look at how Joe's experiences help us better understand the general eschatology of all humanity and creation.

Death and Particular Judgment

Before we can really follow Joe's experience through the "last things," we should know a little about him. Joe was baptized Catholic and thus began his journey of faith. People who knew Joe knew he was Catholic, but he wasn't world-renowned as a saint or a great theologian. In fact, if you ran into Joe on the street you'd think he was pretty average, if you noticed him at all. Joe struggled to faithfully follow Christ to his dying day. Sometimes he stumbled, sometimes he succeeded. But Joe always trusted in Jesus, he celebrated the sacraments, and he did small acts of service in his family and out in the world whenever he could. By earthly means, Joe didn't live a remarkable life, but by trying to live a Christian life and trusting in his faith, Joe was saying "yes" to God every day.

What about those who didn't have the chance to hear the gospel or be baptized? The Catholic Church teaches us that God desires the salvation of everyone and has provided for the salvation of the whole world through the death and resurrection of Jesus:

"The Holy Spirit offers to all the possibility of being made partakers, in a way known to God, of the Paschal mystery. Every man who is ignorant of the Gospel of Christ and of his Church, but seeks the truth and does the will of God in accordance with his understanding of it, can be saved" (CCC 1260).

TEENS

© 2023 Liguori Publications. Photocopying prohibited

CCC 670–682, 954–59, 988–1001, 1020–1065, 1260, 2820

Eschatology: the "Last Things"

- Discuss the introductory questions as a group. Be prepared to share your own responses.
- As you define eschatology, allow time for participants to ask questions and clarify them before you move forward in the lesson.

Death and Particular Judgment

- As you read through this section, make sure to discuss the sidebar and what the Church teaches about those who aren't baptized or haven't heard the Gospel.
- Ask students how they'd explain "particular judgment" and the Church's teaching on God and salvation. Use this time to clarify confusion before moving forward.

Suggested responses include: it is "particular" judgment because it deals with each of us individually, it is when God judges the choices we've made in our lives, and it is when we find out if we're going to purgatory, heaven, or hell.

Heaven

- Discuss participants' imagined view of heaven. Stress that this is a mystery of faith beyond our understanding.
- If you have time, you may want to read some verses from the *CCC* with participants about heaven and discuss them as a group.

Suggested verses include: 1024 (perfect life with the Most Holy Trinity); 1025 (to be one with Christ); and 1029 (we will continue to fulfill God's will).

Hell

- Emphasize that God doesn't predestine or force people to go to hell. God offers each person a choice, and those who eventually wind up in hell end up there because they *finally and definitively* chose to reject God.
- If you have time, you may want to read some verses from the *CCC* with participants about hell and discuss them as a group.

Suggested verses include: 1033 (if we refuse to repent and accept God's mercy we remain separate from him), 1035 (the chief punishment of hell is separation from God), and 1037 (God does not predestine anyone to hell).

Purgatory

- Emphasize that purgatory is a real and possible experience for many, but that this is a merciful provision of a loving God.
- Ask participants to explain purgatory in their own words. Clarify misunderstandings.
- If you have time, you may want to read some verses from the *CCC* with participants about purgatory and discuss them as a group.

Suggested verses include: 1030 (if we are in God's grace, but imperfect, we go to purgatory); and 1031 (Purgatory is entirely different from hell).

This life, and its opportunity to receive salvation, eventually comes to an end. "Death puts an end to human life as the time open to either accepting or rejecting the divine grace manifested in Christ" (*CCC* 1021). When Joe dies, he immediately faces divine judgment. "Just as it is appointed that human beings die once, and after this the judgment" (Hebrews 9:27). This is called the "particular judgment" because it is given to each individual person.

There are three possible outcomes of Joe's judgment:

1. He could be granted immediate entrance into the joy of heaven.
2. He could enter heaven after going through a final purification in purgatory.
3. He could be condemned to hell.

The basis of Joe's judgment is love. Did Joe repent and accept the love of God and respond by loving God and others? Did he accept God's mercy and grace, or did he refuse it?

- *How would you explain the particular judgment to someone else?*
- *What does the Catholic Church teach about God and salvation?*

Heaven, Hell, or Purgatory?

Heaven

Heaven: "the ultimate end and fulfillment of the deepest human longings, the state of supreme, definitive happiness" (*CCC* 1024).

If Joe dies "in God's grace and friendship...perfectly purified," his soul goes straight to heaven (*CCC* 1023). Heaven is a place of joy because we see the beauty of God. In heaven, we experience the fullness of communion with the Holy Trinity, Mary, the saints, our departed loved ones, and all the citizens of heaven. Scripture and tradition use all kinds of images to describe it—a heavenly city, a glorious wedding banquet, a beautiful paradise—but these images can only point toward that supreme happiness which is beyond human understanding.

- *What do you imagine heaven will be like?*

Hell

If Joe had rejected God's mercy and died in mortal sin without repenting, he would separate himself from God eternally and end up in **hell**. How, and why, is this even possible? God loves everyone, but he also gives us the freedom to receive or reject his love. This means each individual has the ultimate choice. Finally and definitively choosing to reject God leads to eternal separation from God: hell. "God predestines no one to go to hell; for this a willing turning away from God (a mortal sin) is necessary" (*CCC* 1037).

Purgatory

What if Joe has responded to God's mercy but at death was not completely free from all attachments to sin? What if Joe was still imperfect when he died? He can be "assured of eternal salvation" but must go through "purification" after death to "achieve the holiness necessary to enter the joy of heaven" (*CCC* 1030). This final purification is called **purgatory**. From the day of our baptism forward, God is working in our lives to "purge" us from sin. If that process is not complete by the time of our death, God completes it after we die.

Scripture encourages us to pray for the dead, and this includes the souls in purgatory (2 Maccabees 12:44). We believe that the living members of the Church on earth, the saints in heaven, and the souls in purgatory are united as one Mystical Body in Christ, and we help one another through mutual prayer (*CCC* 954–959).

Praying for the Dead

There is a great comfort in praying for our loved ones who have died. Try praying this prayer for someone you know and love who has died: *Eternal rest grant unto [name] O Lord. And let perpetual light shine upon [him/her]. And may the souls of all the faithful departed, through the mercy of God, rest in peace. Amen.*

The Second Coming of Christ

In the Nicene Creed, Catholics confess that Christ "will come again in glory." Having defeated evil by his death and resurrection and having ascended to heaven, Christ already rules in glory as king. His reign is budding forth, and "God's plan has entered into its fulfillment" (*CCC* 670). However, the Church on earth, and creation itself, awaits its full redemption. We still anticipate the complete perfection of Christ's kingdom when he returns, and sin and death will be no more.

What Is the Rapture?

Some Christians expect the Second Coming to come in two phases:

1. a rapture (or catching up) of all Christians to heaven, followed by
2. a time of tribulation on earth until Christ finally comes again.

This is not the teaching of the Catholic Church. Scripture teaches that the living will meet the Lord "in the clouds" as he descends to earth. This catching up of the faithful and Christ's Second Coming are not two distinct events but one (see 1 Thessalonians 4:16–17). Some Christians also expect an earthly thousand-year reign of Christ after his Second Coming. This is based on a literal interpretation of Revelation 20, which the Catholic Church rejects.

The Resurrection of the Body

When Christ comes again, he will raise the dead. Joe's soul will be reunited to his body, which will be miraculously raised and transformed by God's infinite power. Many religions and philosophies believe that some spiritual part of the human being will survive after death. The Christian faith goes further and proclaims that the power of death over humanity has been conquered by the resurrection of Jesus. Consequently, the whole human person (body and soul) will be restored for eternal life. We will live forever with God in some beautiful form that will never age, decay, or suffer. This belief is beyond human understanding, but Christ's transfiguration and post-resurrection appearances, as well as his presence in the Eucharist, give us a glimpse.

- *How do you envision your resurrected body? Does this knowledge change the way you feel about your current body?*

INQUIRY

JOURNEY OF FAITH

The Final Judgment

The Final Judgment comes after the resurrection of the dead. "In the presence of Christ, who is Truth itself, the truth of man's relationship with God will be laid bare" (*CCC* 1039). Joe's particular judgment determined his eternal destiny and will not change. But in the **Final Judgment**, all our actions and their consequences will be known, and their ultimate meaning within the context of God's saving work throughout the ages will be revealed to all humankind. Christ will pronounce judgment on every evil act and reward every good deed with the honor it deserves (see John 5:21–29).

- *When you think about the Final Judgment, does it motivate you to change anything about the way you live your life now?*

The End

After all this, at the very end, Joe will enjoy eternal life in the new heaven and a new earth (see Isaiah 65:17, 2 Peter 3:13, and Revelation 21:1). Not only humanity but also the entire universe and all creation will be redeemed—transformed in some marvelous manner to share in eternal life.

Waiting for this end shouldn't remove our motivation to improve this present world. On the contrary, faith and hope motivates us to serve others and work for the "world's" renewal here and now as a sign and beginning of its perfection through Christ (*CCC* 1049, 2820).

Q16

The Resurrection of the Body

- Give participants time to answer the reflection question on their own, and then discuss as a group. You may consider reading 1 Corinthians 15:40–49 (which describes the heavenly, resurrected body) to help participants understand the resurrected body even further.

The Final Judgment

- Discuss the difference between "particular judgment" and the "Last Judgment."

Particular judgment happens when we die and is when our souls enter heaven immediately or after purification, or refuse God's mercy and end up in hell (CCC 1022).

The Last Judgment refers to Christ's return and the triumph of God's justice over all the injustices of the world (CCC 1038), the resurrection of the body, and the reunification of body and soul (see CCC 1059–60).

With a partner or as a group, try to find references to God's kingdom in the Bible. Share what you find. Based on these examples, what do you think the kingdom of God will look like? *Encourage students to think not just about physical characteristics but about how people will treat each other, what people will do, and more.*

Suggested Scripture and responses include: John 18:36 (the kingdom does not belong to this world); Romans 14:17 (righteousness, peace, and joy in the Holy Spirit); Luke 17:20–21 (it cannot be observed, it is among us); and Daniel 2:44 (it will stand forever).

INQUIRY

JOURNEY OF FAITH

With a partner or as a group, try to find references to God's kingdom in the Bible.

Share what you find. Based on these examples, what do you think the kingdom of God will look like?

Think of three things you can do to prepare yourself and others for death, judgment, and the coming of Christ.

Journey of Faith for Teens: Inquiry, Q16 (826337)

The process by which adults are initiated into the Catholic faith throughout the United States is now called the OCIA—the Order of Christian Initiation of Adults. "Order" is a clearer translation of the Latin term for the process formerly known as the RCIA—the Rite of Christian Initiation of Adults. People preparing for baptism and reception into the Church celebrate several rites as part of the order to which those rites belong—an order whose mission is to journey in the faith. The US Conference of Catholic Bishops adopted the name change in 2021, with American dioceses introducing the name thereafter. For more information, please contact your local diocese.

Imprimi Potest: Stephen T. Rehrauer, CSsR, Provincial, Denver Province, the Redemptorists.

Imprimatur: "In accordance with CIC 827, permission to publish has been granted on March 29, 2016, by the Most Reverend Edward M. Rice, Auxiliary Bishop, Archdiocese of St. Louis. Permission to publish is an indication that nothing contrary to Church teaching is contained in this work. It does not imply any endorsement of the opinions expressed in the publication; nor is any liability assumed by this permission."

Journey of Faith for Teens © 2000, 2016 Liguori Publications, Liguori, MO 63057. All rights reserved. No part of this publication may be reproduced, distributed, stored, transmitted, or posted in any form by any means without prior written permission. To order, visit Liguori.org or call 800-325-9521. Liguori Publications, a nonprofit corporation, is an apostolate of the Redemptorists. To learn more about the Redemptorists, visit Redemptorists.com.

© 2023 Liguori Publications. Photocopying prohibited

Editors of 2016 edition: Theresa Nienaber and Pat Fosarelli, MD, DMin. Design: Lorena Mitre Jimenez. Images: Shutterstock.

Scripture texts in this work are taken from the *New American Bible*, revised edition ©2010, 1991, 1986, 1970 Confraternity of Christian Doctrine, Washington, D.C., and are used by permission of the copyright owner. All Rights Reserved. No part of the New American Bible may be reproduced in any form without permission in writing from the copyright owner. Excerpts from English translation of the *Catechism of the Catholic Church* for the United States of America © 1994 United States Catholic Conference, Inc. —*Libreria Editrice Vaticana*; English translation of the Catechism of the Catholic Church: Modifications from the Editio Typica © 1997 United States Catholic Conference, Inc. —*Libreria Editrice Vaticana*. Compliant with *The Roman Missal, Third Edition*.

Printed in the United States of America.
Third Edition.

Liguori PUBLICATIONS
A Redemptorist Ministry

Journey of Faith

Journaling

Think of three things you can do to prepare yourself and others for death, judgment, and the coming of Christ.

Closing Prayer

Close with a recitation of the Lord's Prayer, with particular focus on the words "thy kingdom come."

Looking Ahead

Over the next few days, encourage participants to spend time in prayer for the souls in purgatory.

Journey of Faith for Teens
Inquiry Glossary (alphabetical)

Advent: The beginning of the liturgical year. It begins on the fourth Sunday before Christmas and ends before the first evening prayer of Christmas on Christmas Eve. This season emphasizes the coming (advent or arrival) of Jesus Christ, joy, hope, repentance, expectation, and preparation. The first part of Advent highlights his Second Coming at the end of time, and the second part (December 17–24) his coming into human history by his birth.

alb: A Latin word for "white," this long white garment is symbolic of the total purity that should cover one in one's approach to God. It is worn by the celebrant (priest), a deacon, and even those who serve as lectors, servers, acolytes, or other lay ministers.

alleluia: Meaning "praise the Lord" in Hebrew, this word is used frequently during the Easter season and is recited or sung before the reading of the Gospel (except during Lent) to emphasize the presence of Jesus in the word of God.

altar: The central table on which the Communion bread and the cup of wine are offered as the eucharistic sacrifice. The altar "represents the two aspects of the same mystery: the altar of the sacrifice and the table of the Lord" (*CCC* 1383).

altar server: Assists at the altar during liturgies by carrying the cross or processional candles, holding the book for the celebrant when needed, carrying the incense and censer, presenting the bread, wine, and water during the preparation of the gifts, washing the hands of the priest, and any other necessary tasks. Altar servers can be male or female but must have received their first Communion prior to participating as a server.

ambo: An elevated pulpit from which the Scriptures are proclaimed during Mass.

Ascension (of the Lord): One of the principal feast days of the Christian year, it occurs on the fortieth day of the Easter season (it is celebrated on the sixth Thursday after Easter or the following Sunday). This feast day marks when Jesus rose (ascended) into heaven.

associate pastor: Also known as parochial vicar, a priest who assists a pastor in the parish (see **pastor**).

Assumption (of Mary): This feast day occurs on August 15 and celebrates Mary's assumption, body and soul, into heaven. It is one of the principal Marian feasts of the Church year and was proclaimed as a dogma by Pope Pius XII on November 1, 1950.

auxiliary bishop: A helper bishop who assists in large dioceses (see **bishop**).

baptismal font: A large basin or small pool that contains the blessed water used for baptizing. Every parish church should have a baptismal font, which is usually set in a prominent and visible place in the church building.

beatified: A person who is beatified has been declared by the pope as someone, now deceased, who has lived a life worthy of public veneration on a limited (not universal) basis in the Church, and is now in heaven. Beatification occurs only after a person's life, virtue, reputation for holiness, ministry, and writings are scrutinized heavily by the Church and after one miracle has been ascribed to him or her. A person who has been beatified is called "Blessed."

Bible: Also called sacred Scripture or the Scriptures, it is a collection of books accepted by the Church as the inspired, authentic account of God's self-revelation and plan of salvation for the human race. It is divided into the Old Testament and New Testament. (See **Old Testament and New Testament**.)

bishop: The chief pastor and head of a specific diocese. According to the Second Vatican Council, the bishop is called to "eminently and visibly take the place of Christ himself, teacher, shepherd and priest, and act in his person" (Dogmatic Constitution on the Church *[Lumen Gentium]*, 21).

brother (religious): A man who is a member of a religious order but is not ordained. The *Catechism* states that religious life is "one way of experiencing a 'more intimate' consecration, rooted in Baptism and dedicated totally to God" (*CCC* 916).

canonization: The final declaration by the pope that a person is a saint, in heaven, and worthy of veneration by all the faithful. This step is normally preceded by beatification and the authentication of two miracles ascribed to him or her by the Church (see **beatified**).

cantor: A member of the church choir who leads the congregation in song.

cardinal: Canon law describes the cardinals as those who "constitute a special college which provides for the election of the Roman Pontiff...The cardinals assist the Roman Pontiff either collegially...or individually when they help the Roman Pontiff through the various offices they perform" (*Canon* 349). Cardinal is an honorary title, and cardinals are normally bishops.

catechism: A summary or manual containing the basics of Christian doctrine. The *Catechism of the Catholic Church* was commissioned by a synod of bishops in 1986 and first published in English in 1994 for the purpose of "faithfully and systematically present[ing] the teaching of Sacred Scripture, the living Tradition of the Church and the authentic Magisterium" *(Fidei Depositum).*

catechist: Someone who instructs and forms others in the Catholic faith either in preparation for baptism or continuing instruction and formation for those who are already baptized.

catechumenate: The period of instruction and involvement in the Catholic faith in preparation for the baptism of adults or for the reception of baptized non-Catholics. Those preparing to receive baptism and admission into the Church are called catechumens.

celibacy: In general, the unmarried state of life. Celibacy is a vocation in which one freely chooses to be unmarried "for the sake of the kingdom of heaven" (Matthew 19:12). This vocation may be lived in a lay state or in a religious institute. Celibacy is required of candidates for the priesthood, with the exception of married men ordained in another tradition.

chasuble: The outermost garment worn by the priest in the celebration of Mass.

Christmas: Also called the feast of the Nativity of the Lord, celebrated on December 25. Many of the customs surrounding Christmas have origins in pagan celebrations but have been "christened" with religious significance.

Church: The visible religious society founded by Jesus Christ under St. Peter and his successors. The purpose of the Church is to preserve and proclaim Jesus' teachings and to make present his sacrifice and sacraments for the salvation of all.

Church hierarchy: The systematic arrangement of authority within the Catholic Church. It can refer to the hierarchy of holy orders (bishops, priests, or deacons) as well as the hierarchy of jurisdiction (the pope and the bishops).

Church year: Beginning with the first Sunday of Advent, followed by the Christmas season, Ordinary Time, Lent, the Easter Triduum, the Easter season, and ending with Ordinary Time, this calendar "unfolds the whole mystery of Christ" (Constitution on the Sacred Liturgy [*Sacrosanctum Concilium*], 102; see **Advent, Christmas, Ordinary Time, Lent, Triduum, Easter**).

cloister: Residences of men or women religious that restrict the free entry of outsiders to promote a life of prayer and reflection for the religious who live there.

conclave: The enclosure of the cardinals in Rome while electing a new pope. The conclave was instituted by Gregory X in 1274 to avoid interference from the outside world during the election of a pope.

confessional: The place in a church set aside for celebration of the sacrament of penance. The penitent has the option of confessing to the priest face to face or anonymously behind a screen.

consecration: The moment when the bread and wine are changed into the Body and Blood of our Lord. According to the *Catechism,* "The Eucharistic presence of Christ begins at the moment of the consecration and endures as long as the Eucharistic species subsist" (*CCC* 1377).

convent: The building housing a community of religious sisters.

crucifix: A cross with the image of Jesus as suffering Savior. Catholics find the blessed crucifix a revered object of private or public devotion as a reminder of the triumphant suffering of Christ.

dalmatic: An outer liturgical garment worn by a deacon at Mass.

deacon: A member of the clergy who is ordained for service to the people of God, ranked under bishops and priests. The role of the deacon is to serve the corporal and spiritual needs of the community and to assist in preaching the word of God. There are two types of deacons: transitional and permanent. (See **transitional deacon** and **permanent deacon**.)

diocese: "A community of the Christian faithful in communion of faith and sacraments with the bishop ordained in apostolic succession" (*CCC* 833). A diocese serves a specific geographical area and is led by a bishop. Parishes make up a diocese and are led by pastors.

diocesan priest: A priest who is ordained into the service of a diocese and commits himself to a certain geographical area.

divine revelation: God's self-revelation to humankind. Both sacred Scripture and tradition are part of divine revelation.

divinely inspired: The books of the Bible are considered divinely inspired because their authors were inspired to write through the grace and help of the Holy Spirit.

dogma: An official teaching of the Church, defined by the Magisterium. The *Catechism* states that "the Church's Magisterium exercises the authority it holds from Christ to the fullest extent when it defines dogmas, that is, when it proposes truths contained in divine Revelation or also when it proposes...truths having a necessary connection with them" (*CCC* 88).

Easter: A movable feast celebrated on a Sunday between March 22 and April 25. This feast celebrates the resurrection of Jesus Christ from the dead. It is considered the greatest of all Christian feasts; the Easter season continues for fifty days from Easter to the feast of Pentecost. (See *CCC* 1170).

Easter candle: A large candle symbolic of the risen Savior, the Light of the World. It is blessed on Holy Saturday and remains lit throughout the Easter season during liturgical services.

epistles: Also called letters, they make up a large part of the New Testament. The epistles are commonly divided into the Pauline letters and the Catholic letters. The Pauline letters were written by St. Paul or by his disciples in his name. The Catholic letters were written to a more universal audience by various authors from AD 65 to about 95.

eschatology: Greek for "last things," this is the part of theology focused on the last things of death, judgment, heaven, hell, purgatory, the resurrection of the body, and the Second Coming of Christ.

Eucharist: This word means "thanksgiving." It is one of the sacraments of the Church and is the source and summit of all Christian worship and life. The sacrament of the Eucharist was instituted by Jesus at the Last Supper and is celebrated by the Church today. During the Eucharist, the offering of bread and wine becomes the precious Body and Blood of Christ.

extraordinary minister of holy Communion: Someone who is delegated to administer the Eucharist after it has been consecrated by a priest or the celebrant.

faith: Both a grace and the human act of knowing and living like we are loved and cherished by God. The *Catechism* expands on this by saying that "'Faith *seeks understanding*'; it is intrinsic to faith that the believer desires to know better the One in whom he has put his faith....The grace of faith opens 'the eyes of your hearts' to a lively understand of the contents of Revelation" (*CCC* 154).

feast (day): Days designated for remembrance and celebration of a saint, holy person, or event that has special significance to the Church.

Final Judgment: As spoken of in the New Testament, the Final or General Judgment is the final encounter with Christ at his Second Coming during which all of humanity will be judged.

Gloria: An ancient hymn of praise that begins with the song of the angels from St. Luke's account of the birth of Christ.

godparent: Someone who is chosen by the candidate being baptized or parents of the child being baptized to serve as a mentor in the faith. A godparent must be at least sixteen years old, an actively practicing Catholic, and willing to take on the commitment of walking alongside the newly baptized on the road of Christian life.

Gospel: Meaning "good news," a Gospel is one of the four divinely inspired accounts of the life, teaching, suffering, death, and resurrection of Jesus Christ. The Gospels include the books of Matthew, Mark, Luke, and John.

hallowed: To recognize and treat something as holy, or to give honor or reverence to.

heaven: Eternal life with God and the saints. Heaven is the ultimate goal of human life.

hell: A state of "definitive self-exclusion from communion with God and the blessed" (*CCC* 1033). To be in hell after death requires someone to die in mortal sin and the free choice to refuse to repent and the rejection God's merciful love.

Holy, Holy, Holy: A song of praise to God taken from the Book of Isaiah that begins the Eucharistic Prayer.

holy days of obligation: Days set aside for the worship of God. This includes each Sunday of the year and other feast days designated by the Church. All Catholics are required to participate in the Mass on these days.

Holy See: Also referred to as the Apostolic See, it can mean the official residence of the pope or the power of the pope as supreme pontiff. It also includes the tribunals and congregations that assist the pope in Church governance.

holy water: Water that is blessed by a priest for use by Catholics. It is used most often to make the sign of the cross while blessing oneself. Holy water is a reminder of baptism and symbolic of spiritual cleansing.

Holy Week: The week before Easter beginning with Palm (Passion) Sunday and including the Easter Triduum of Holy Thursday, Good Friday, and the Easter Vigil (see **Triduum**.)/

homily: Usually, but not always, given by the presider of the Mass, it is an instruction or sermon that seeks to explain the day's Scripture readings and how to apply them meaningfully to the lives of people today.

honor: To hold someone in great respect or high regard.

immaculate conception: The belief that the Virgin Mary was preserved by a singular grace and privilege from sin at the first instance of her conception. The feast of Mary's Immaculate Conception is celebrated as a holy day of obligation in the Church on December 8.

inerrant: The attributes of the books of Scripture whereby they faithfully and without error teach the truth which God, for the sake of our salvation, wished to have confided through the sacred Scriptures. (See *CCC* 107)

infallibility: The teaching that the Church, through the power of God, is preserved from the possibility and liability of error in teaching matters of faith and morals. This also means that under certain conditions, the teaching of the pope is without error through the power of the Holy Spirit.

introductory rites: These are the rites that begin the Mass and include: the entrance chant or song, the Sign of the Cross and a greeting from the celebrant, the penitential act, the *Gloria*, and an opening prayer. Following these introductory rites is the Liturgy of the Word.

inquiry: The first stage of the OCIA. In this stage, the inquirer is learning about Christ, the Church, prayer, the saints, and the Christian way of life. The purpose of this stage is for the inquirer to grow and develop in faith and to determine if he or she desires to move forward in the OCIA process.

laity: Those members of the Church who are not ordained in holy orders. The laity are called to witness the faith with their lives.

lectern: A wood or metal podium from which all nonscriptural readings and singing are led.

Lectionary: A book containing a three-year cycle of Scripture readings for Sundays and some feasts, a two-year weekday cycle, a one-year cycle for saints feast days, and readings for ritual Masses and Masses for particular intentions.

lector: Someone who proclaims the Scripture readings, except for the Gospels, in liturgical worship.

Lent: The penitential season beginning on Ash Wednesday and ending before the Mass on Holy Thursday.

liturgical year: See **Church year**

liturgy: The official public worship of the Church. It includes the celebration of the sacrament and sacrifice of the Eucharist and the celebration of the other sacraments.

Liturgy of the Eucharist: The second main part of the eucharistic celebration of the Latin rite. It begins with the presentation of the bread and wine and prayers of offering by the priest, next the priest recites a prayer of thanksgiving, the congregation responds with the "Holy, Holy, Holy," and the Eucharistic Prayer. This is followed by the Communion rite, final prayers, and the sending forth of the people.

Liturgy of the Word: The first main part of the eucharistic celebration of the Latin rite. It includes the proclamation of the word of God, a homily on the Scriptures, the recitation of the Creed, and the offering of petitions.

magisterium: Latin for "teaching authority," this authority is vested in the pope and the bishops in union with him. This teaching authority is sometimes infallible, and it always expresses authentic Catholic teaching. For this reason, all Catholics are called to be faithful and loyal to these teachings.

Mass: A time when the children of God gather to give thanks and praise to God, listen to the word of the Lord through sacred Scripture, and are nourished by Christ's Body and Blood in holy Communion.

Messiah: A Hebrew word meaning "savior" or "deliverer" and used as a title of Jesus, the Son of God.

miracle: A sign or wonder, such as healing or the control of nature, which can only be attributed to divine power. The miracles of Jesus were messianic signs of the presence of God's kingdom.

monastery: A place where religious live in seclusion from the outside world. It can be applied to religious communities of both men and women but is commonly used to describe the home of monks or other religious men who live a cloistered life.

monk: A male religious who is a member of a monastic community. Common monastic orders in the Church include: the Benedictines, the Cistercians, and the Carthusians.

monstrance: A sacred vessel constructed of precious metals in such a way that the consecrated host is clearly visible. It is used when the consecrated host is exposed for eucharistic adoration or a eucharistic procession.

music minister: Those who help to lead music during the liturgy.

mystagogy: This is the final stage of the OCIA, which continues until Pentecost and is a period of post-baptismal catechesis. The purpose of mystagogy is to allow the newly baptized to reflect on their baptism, learn more about their new faith, and explore the ways they may be called to serve the Church in the world and their parish.

Mystical Body: Another name for the Catholic Church. The Church is "mystical" because the Church is a mystery revealed by God which must be accepted on faith. The Church is a "body" because the Church is the body of Christ present on earth.

Nativity (of the Lord): The Nativity of the Lord refers to the birth of Jesus Christ in Bethlehem. It is celebrated on December 25 (see **Christmas**).

New Testament: Contains twenty-seven books written in Greek between AD 50 and 140. It includes the four Gospels, the Acts of the Apostles, the epistles of St. Paul, other epistles, and the Book of Revelation. The major theme of the New Testament is Jesus Christ: his person, preaching, saving death and resurrection, and relationship to us.

nun: While commonly used to describe any female religious, this term actually applies only to those who live the monastic life or in a cloister that restricts contact with the outside world.

offertory: When the unconsecrated bread and wine are brought to the altar and prepared as an offering to God.

Old Testament: Contains forty-six books written in Hebrew between the years 900 BC and 160 BC. Included are books with distinct purposes: historical, moral, and prophetic. These books are a record of God's dealing with the Israelites, "the Chosen People," and of their responses to the divine plan.

Ordinary Time: The period in the liturgical year between the end of the Christmas season and the beginning of Lent, and the Monday after Pentecost until the beginning of Advent.

ordination: The process of priestly authority being passed down, through the laying on of hands, from one generation to the next. Ordination takes place during the sacrament of holy orders, which has three forms: the diaconate (deacons), priesthood (priests), and the episcopate (bishops).

paschal candle: (See **Easter candle**.)

parish: A geographical area within a diocese that has been assigned its own church and pastor.

parish council: A group of parishioners who advise and assist the pastor in the work of the parish.

pastor: According to canon law, "The pastor is the proper (shepherd) of the parish entrusted to him, exercising the pastoral care of the community committed to him under the authority of the diocesan bishop in whose ministry of Christ he has been called to share...he carries out the functions of teaching, sanctifying, and governing, also with the cooperation of other presbyters or deacons and with the assistance of lay members of the Christian faithful" (*Canon* 519; see also **associate pastor**).

pastoral administrator: A man or woman who shares some administrative duties of a parish with the pastor. This is an administrative, not liturgical, role and the celebration of Mass and the sacraments still falls to a priest.

permanent deacon: A married or unmarried man who is ordained a deacon and remains a deacon permanently. To become a permanent deacon a man must be (1) qualified, unmarried, and twenty-five years of age or older or (2) qualified, married, and age thirty-five or older with the consent of his wife. Once ordained a permanent deacon a man cannot marry (if unmarried) or remarry (if married).

person: When used in reference to the Holy Trinity, person refers to one of the three persons of God: Father, Son, or Holy Spirit.

petitions: See **Universal Prayer**

pope: This is the title of the bishop of Rome, the successor of St. Peter, the apostle Jesus named as the head of the apostles and the head of the Church. As head of the Church, the pope leads as shepherd all the faithful in his care.

prayer: Raising one's heart and mind to God. There are many ways to pray and we are called to participate in both private prayer and prayer as part of our Church community. Different types of prayer include blessing and adoration, petition, intercession, thanksgiving, praise, and contrition.

priest: A man who is ordained through the sacrament of holy orders to serve the faithful. He has the authority to perform the sacraments and celebrate the Mass.

Purgatory: The transitional state where those souls that have been judged worthy of heaven but are imperfect at the time of death will undergo a final purification.

purification and enlightenment: This is the third period of the OCIA and the final period leading up to the Easter Vigil and reception of the sacraments. This period emphasizes prayer by both those seeking initiation into the Church and the parish community, as well as a further opportunity for study and spiritual direction.

OCIA: The Order of Christian Initiation of Adults is the process of becoming a member of the Catholic Church for those past the age of reason. The order begins with a participant's entry into the catechumenate and culminates in the celebration of the sacraments of initiation.

Reconciliation Room: See **confessional**

rectory: The residence of the priests serving a parish.

religious order: Organized groups of religious who live and work together under a unique charism and with a specific ministries in which members take part (prayer, service, teaching, health care, and so on). Those in a religious order generally take vows of poverty, chastity, and obedience.

religious priest: Unlike a diocesan priest, a religious priest belongs to a religious community and usually lives with his community rather than in the parish. Religious priests also take the same vows as others in their religious order including vows of poverty, chastity, and obedience.

responsorial psalm: A psalm (which almost always comes from the Book of Psalms) sung or recited during Mass between the first and second readings at on Sundays and major feast days, or between the first reading and the Gospel on other days.

***Roman Missal, The*:** Also called the *Sacramentary*, this is a book of prayers and directives for the celebration of the Mass and other sacraments.

rosary: A meditation on the events (called "Mysteries") in the life of Jesus and Mary includes the Joyful, Sorrowful, Glorious, and Luminous.

sacraments of initiation: The sacraments received to become a full member of the Catholic Church: baptism, confirmation, and the Eucharist.

(sacred) Tradition: Coming from the apostles through the teachings of Jesus, Tradition works closely with Scripture to transmit the Word of God in its entirety to the world. "Through Tradition, 'the Church, in her doctrine, life, and worship perpetuates and transmits to every generation all that she herself is and all that she believes'" (see *CCC* 74–100).

sacristy: A room near or in the church used to store sacred vessels and other materials used in the liturgy. This room is also used by the priest and other church ministers to prepare for Mass and other services.

saint: A person who has lived a holy life, is in heaven, and is honored by the universal Church (see **beatified** and **canonization**).

salvation history: The history of God's interactions with humankind during the course of revelation.

sanctuary: The area in the front or near the center of the church where the altar, lectern, tabernacle, and sometimes the baptismal font are located.

sanctuary lamp: A light or candle kept burning at all times whenever the Blessed Sacrament is present. This light can usually be found near the tabernacle.

Scriptures: See **Bible**

scrutinies: Three additional rites during the third, fourth, and fifth Sundays of Lent for the unbaptized elect. The purpose of these scrutinies is to examine one's life and to reflect on personal sin through the light of God's mercy and grace.

sister (religious): A woman who is a member of a religious order. The *Catechism* states that religious life is "one way of experiencing a 'more intimate' consecration, rooted in baptism and dedicated totally to God" (*CCC* 916).

sponsor: It is the sponsor's role to offer support and encouragement during the OCIA process and then to present the candidate when it is time for them to receive the sacraments. The requirements for a sponsor are the same as for a godparent.

Stations of the Cross: Also called the Way of the Cross, this is a devotion in honor of the passion and death of Christ. It consists of meditation on the stations of the passion from Jesus' condemnation to the laying in the tomb. Many churches have pictorial stations or crosses attached to the walls around the church depicting each scene.

stole: A thin band of material worn around the neck and shoulders, symbolic of the "yoke of the Lord." Priests wear a stole during the celebration of all the sacraments. Deacons may also wear a stole, but only diagonally over the shoulder.

substance: In a spiritual context, substance describes what God is, a being whose essence requires that it exist in itself rather than a being that exists in or because of another.

tabernacle: A special place where the consecrated Eucharist is kept. The tabernacle should be located in a visible and prominent place in the church.

testament: A formal agreement or covenant used to describe the relationship between God and his Chosen People.

Torah: Also known as the Pentateuch, this is the name given to the first five books of the Bible: Genesis, Exodus, Leviticus, Numbers, and Deuteronomy.

transitional deacon: A man who receives the order of deacon as he advances to the priesthood.

Triduum: The Easter Triduum is the central celebration of the Church year and includes the three celebrations leading up to Easter: Holy Thursday, Good Friday, and Holy Saturday.

Trinity: The doctrine that states there are three persons in one God, the Father, Son, and Holy Spirit, and that they are eternally united in a communion of love.

Universal Prayer: The offering of prayers to God by the faithful during Mass. These prayers usually include petitions for the holy Church, those who govern the Church, those suffering for various needs, the community, and the world.

vestments: Symbolic garments worn by priests and deacons during liturgical celebrations.

worship: Due to God alone, worship is an act of adoration and submission to the one who created the world and the one who gives us eternal life.